Real Estate
the Ethical Way

Bob Hunt, CRB

Foreword by Blanche Evans

Bella Vista Publishing Company, Inc.

Managing editor: Barbara Cox
Copy editor: Joe Tinervia

Library of Congress Cataloging-in-Publication Data

Hunt, Robert, 1937-
Real estate the ethical way / by Bob Hunt.
p. cm.
Includes bibliographical references and index.
ISBN-13: 978-0-9718225-3-5 (pbk.)
ISBN-10: 0-9718225-3-0 (pbk.)
1. Real estate agents—Professional ethics. 2. Real estate business—
Moral and ethical aspects. I. Title.

HD1382.H86 2008
174'.933333
2007048803

Bella Vista Publishing Company, Inc.
San Clemente, CA 92672

Printed in the United States of America.
10 9 8 7 6 5 4 3 2 1
ISBN-10: 0-9718225-3-0
ISBN-13: 978-0-9718225-3-5

For Nancy Hunt

Not only the best person, but also the best Realtor®

Bob Hunt

———————

Acknowledgments

I could not begin to do an adequate job of acknowledging and thanking the many people who have contributed to the writing of this book. Chief among them, of course, are my family members—children, in-laws, and grandchildren—who have been tolerant of my quirky habits and who have forgiven the fact that "Grampy" has sometimes been upstairs writing, when he should have been tending to the barbecue.

Chris Read, Scott Brunner, and Cliff Niersbach were kind enough to read the manuscript and to comment on it. It is a better book because of them. It should be needless to say, but I'll say it: errors and problems that remain are entirely my fault, and none of theirs.

This book is the result of thoughts and attempts to articulate those thoughts that have occurred over the course of what pretty much constitutes a career in real estate. During the course of that career, I have done a fair amount of writing, and some very kind people have encouraged me in those endeavors. For that encouragement, I particularly want to thank Glen Hellyer, one of the more astute Realtors® I have known; Jeff Tiss, a title company representative who has demonstrated that you can be successful while playing by the rules; and Cherri Jessup, a dear friend and a Realtor® with heart. Their words of encouragement have meant more than they will ever know.

Our son, Matt, of Saddleback College, and Barbara Cox of Bella Vista Publishing have put their doctorates to work by helping to make this book both more readable and more grammatically correct. Their encouragement has meant a great deal to me, and they have also been a lot of fun to work with. Whatever blemishes remain should be held to my account, not theirs.

I owe thanks, and perhaps apologies, to many of the good agents at our office—particularly our son, Scott—who allowed me to test some of these scenarios on their sensibilities. My partner and friend, David Silver-Westrick, has been both patient and helpful as I have tested a variety of these ideas on him. I sincerely appreciate his insights and his forbearance.

The contributions of Nancy, my wife, have been invaluable. Her instincts are invariably on target.

Table of Contents

Foreword

Who would have ever dreamed that a book on real estate ethics would be fun to read?

As Realty Times readers already know, Bob Hunt is a great columnist who gives practical advice with humor, empathy and clarity. He gently nudges agents, brokers, and association leaders to pay attention to the latest issues and their potential impacts on the real estate industry.

Both professionally and personally, few Realtors® are as respected and admired as he. You can feel the affection he has for people in his words and his actions. He's a giving, caring man, and I consider it an honor to call him, and his wonderful wife Nancy, my friends.

As a Director for the National Association of Realtors® and the California Association of Realtors®, Bob is the first to see and hear the breaking news that impacts every Realtor®'s business. Lately, changes have been coming fast and furiously.

For many Realtors®, who are simply trying to make a living, so much change is overwhelming. It seems that every time they turn around, there's a new business model to compete against and new language and skills to learn so they can use the latest technologies to work with clients. There are also constant updates to state regulations and to association codes of ethics.

Most agents simply don't have the time or the energy to keep up.

It's this constant sea of change that makes the topic of *ethics* confusing for many working agents. Most people want to do the right thing, but when presented with a tidal wave of choices, it's hard to make the right one.

In this book, you'll learn about everyday situations where an ethical choice has to be made and why. You'll learn which codes to follow when, whether it's the Golden Rule or The Realtor® Code of Ethics, and when to put your own needs or your family's needs first.

So read, relax, and enjoy. You're in good hands. And just from the fact that you picked this book to read means your family and clients are in pretty good hands, too.

Blanche Evans, Realty Times
"Best Real Estate News," Yahoo! Internet Life, March 2002
"Best of the Web: Buying and Selling," Money, June 2003
"Top Reporter Covering NAR," Delahaye-Bacon's, 2005
"25 Most Influential," Realtor Magazine, 2000, 2003, 2006

Introduction

This book is written for Realtors® by a Realtor®. And I am not using "Realtor®" in a generic sense. I am referring to those real estate agents and brokers who are members of the national, state, and local associations of Realtors®. Of course, it would be just fine if non-Realtors® read the book too, especially if they buy it.

Real Estate the Ethical Way is a book written out of experience. I have not personally experienced all of the different types of situations that are described here, but certainly most of them. Moreover, the others have occurred very close by. The names, characters, and settings have, of course, been changed. But the issues are real and, I suspect, repeated many times throughout the country.

The text draws heavily on the Realtor® *Code of Ethics*. In doing so, one of my primary aims has been to help to "demystify" the Code. Every Realtor® is aware of the Code of Ethics. Indeed, by virtue of their membership, they have subscribed to uphold it. Yet, it is my observation that, for many, the Code seems somewhat inaccessible. By that I don't mean that they can't get a copy. Rather I refer to the fact that they view the Code as a document that must be interpreted and explained to them. They know that the Code of Ethics is a good thing, and they agree to adhere to it, but, in their view, understanding and applying the Code to situations is something to be left to the experts—"the people at the Board."

This is unfortunate. It comes about in large part, I believe, because the personal contact that Realtors® have with the Code of Ethics is so infrequent (even though it applies to things that they do on a daily basis). For most, their only contact is either at a hearing—which is a statistically unusual event—or once every four years when their exposure to its history, aims, and various applications occurs in a class that lasts less than three hours. That simply isn't enough exposure for anyone to develop a sense of the Code's intent and applicability. It is hoped that *Real Estate the Ethical Way* can help to make up for such unfamiliarity.

Real Estate the Ethical Way is not organized along the same lines as the Realtor® Code of Ethics is usually presented. Rather, it follows the flow of a Realtor®'s work life (e.g., prospecting, listing, and negotiating). Stories are told about ethically charged situations that occur within those groups of activities, and the scenarios are then analyzed from the perspective both of the Realtor® Code of Ethics and also of common ethical principles.

The book certainly doesn't cover all the possible situations that a Realtor® might encounter and that might pose an ethical issue. Nor does it cover all the sections of the Code of Ethics. I have tried to stick to those issues that I thought were central, although they are occasionally introduced in novel contexts.

The text, then, is not meant to be a commentary or a complete exposition of the Realtor® Code of Ethics. Moreover, it is not confined to applications of the Code. There are plenty of real-estate-related activities that have ethical implications but that are simply not addressed by the Code of Ethics. In such cases, we need to apply general ethical principles as well.

Additionally, there are times when agents and brokers are faced with the occurrence or possibility of activities that are prohibited by law. It is true that some acts that are against the law (e.g., discrimination in housing) are also prohibited by the Code. But not every illegal real estate activity is prohibited by the Code. It does not contain a general rule that says, "Thou shalt obey the law." So, there are law-breaking real estate activities that pose ethical problems for Realtors®, even though those activities may not be addressed by the Code. Some of these are also discussed in this text.

It is my fond hope that this book will be read "in community." That is, I hope that those who read this will share and discuss these issues—perhaps even argue about them—with friends and colleagues in the real estate community. Ethics does not occur in a vacuum. Ethical norms are formed in community. Ethical issues arise and are played out in a community. None of us is a moral Lone Ranger. We need the help and the thoughts of those in our real estate community to discern and to do what is right in the various circumstances we may encounter. I hope that this book will contribute to that joint undertaking.

A Special Note to the Reader

This book does not need to be read serially. That is, you don't have to start at page number one and simply progress page by page. Sure, I had a plan in mind when I wrote it; but you don't have to follow it.

Throughout the book there are occasional references to what has been stated before, but, by and large, each section is quite independent of the others. You should, then, feel free to skip around. If some section strikes you as an area of interest, go ahead and start there. You may then want to go back. That's up to you. But, jump around if you wish. Feel free to go directly to those areas that may be of the most interest to you.

Also, there are frequent references to the Realtor® Code of Ethics, the Standards of Practice, and the Case Interpretations of the Code of Ethics. Those comprise too many pages to reprint here. Realtors® can find them a couple of different ways. One is to obtain a current copy of the *Code of Ethics and Arbitration Manual* either through the National Association of Realtors® (NAR) or at a local association office. Another is to go to the appropriate pages on the NAR website. The Code of Ethics and the Standards of Practice can be found at http://www.realtor.org/MemPolWeb.nsf/pages/Code. The case interpretations are located at http://www.realtor.org/2007CEAM.nsf/Division?OpenView&Start=1&Count=30&Expand=4, which, I admit, is a bit much to copy.

1
Doing the Right Thing

This happened to my wife, Nancy, a long time ago.

A young couple, let's call them Bob and Sandy, made an appointment to meet with her at our office. They wanted to buy a home in our area. They had been referred by mutual friends, the Johnsons. When Nancy met with them it was a bit more complicated than she had anticipated.

Bob and Sandy were clearly upset. They felt caught in a dilemma, and they didn't know what to do. As they explained to Nancy, they had already started looking at homes with another agent. Other friends in their church had suggested that they contact Al. Al was a new agent, recently transitioning from the accounting field. He was a really nice guy, bright enough, and a hard worker. But it just wasn't working.

Bob and Sandy were concerned that Al didn't seem to know very much about real estate. And he wasn't doing a good job of finding a home for them. He only seemed to be familiar with one of the towns in the tri-city area, and he wasn't showing them anything in the other two, even though they had told him that they would be happy in those areas too. Besides that, he just didn't seem to be understanding what it was they were looking for. Maybe no such property existed; or maybe it was their fault. Maybe they were doing a bad job of communicating to him. Whatever it was, he kept showing them things that didn't fit.

Not that he wasn't trying. He had taken them out three different weekends now; and he would call and tell them whenever a new listing came up that he thought they would be interested in. And, as we said, he was a really nice guy.

Bob and Sandy were distressed. What should they do? They had lost all confidence in Al. They wanted Nancy to help them find a home. But they felt they had an obligation to him. He had worked hard and spent a lot of time with them. They felt guilty about just dumping him. They wanted to do what was right.

(Now, let me interrupt this story for just a minute to make a few comments. First of all, remember, this was quite a few years ago. It was long before buyer-broker agreements came into use. Agency disclosure laws hadn't even been written then. So, there were no legal or contractual issues at play.)

Nancy took them out and, in short order, found them a house that they then purchased. She told them that she would handle things with Al, and she told them what she would do.

She called Al and let him know, as gently as possible, what had transpired. She told him that he would receive 50% of her commission as a referral fee at the close of escrow, which he did.

I don't recount this story for the purpose of showing what was or is "the right thing" to do in that or a similar situation. To the contrary. Reasonable, ethical people might disagree. Some might think, "Wait a minute. That's a little overboard. A fruit basket for Al, maybe a gift certificate at a nice restaurant, but 50%? That's crazy. And besides, it rewards incompetent behavior." There might be others who would take the position, "It doesn't matter that there weren't any laws or rules. She should have sent the couple back to Al. He was their agent, and she had no business interfering, even if they did initiate it." Reasonable people, ethical people, could disagree about such things.

Indeed, others might think, "Nancy should have just taken them over, plain and simple. They had no obligation to Al, and neither did she. It might have been nice to have called him, but even that wouldn't have been necessary."

There are many kinds of people in this business, just as there are many different kinds of people in all walks of life. Many of them—I think, I hope, the majority—generally want to do what is right. But they don't always know what the right thing is. And as has been suggested above, it isn't always clear.[1]

---

[1] Moreover, there can be a variety of "right" things—40% would have been a right thing too. Probably even less would have sufficed to be right.

There are others who aren't really bad—they would prefer to do what is right rather than what is wrong—but sometimes, perhaps frequently, they simply do not see that an ethical issue is at stake. They may be unaware of the ethical dimensions of the situations in which they find themselves.

Finally, some just don't care. Whether what they do is right or wrong is of no concern to them. They are motivated by other things.

This book is addressed primarily to the first two groups. Its aim, therefore, is twofold. One goal is to demonstrate to readers the breadth of contexts in which ethical issues may arise in the real estate business. Thus the scenarios in the chapters that follow are set in several categories of activities and relationships that will be familiar to working Realtors®: prospecting, listing, working with buyers, negotiating transactions, etc. The second goal is to provide readers with direction toward being able to determine for themselves, in the various situations they may encounter, the right thing to do. By considering a wide variety of scenarios, and by seeing how various ethical principles apply in those situations, readers should develop not only the ability to spot an ethical issue, but also the ability to deal with it appropriately.

What about the third group, the group that just doesn't care whether what they do is right or wrong? There's not much I can say here. No book—at least no human book—is going to make good guys out of bad guys. There is, though, a brief word of advice that just might be relevant to those who don't care about being ethical: "You might not care, but other people, many other people, do. Indeed, not only clients, but also your broker or manager may care that you act in an ethical way. So you might be well advised to pay attention. Learn how to do the right thing. It could help you keep your job."

Are Real Estate Ethics Different From Other Kinds of Ethics?

A delightful little book by John Maxwell is provocatively titled *There's No Such Thing as Business Ethics.*[2] To be sure, some might be inclined simply to nod in assent and think, "No kidding." But for the curious, or those inclined to disagree, Maxwell's book makes an interesting argument. His point is not that all of business is unethical. Rather, he is disagreeing with the point of view that the operative ethical principles of business are somehow specialized, different from (occasionally, contrary to) the ethical principles that govern our everyday lives.

According to Maxwell, the test of what is ethically acceptable or unacceptable in the business context is exactly the same as that which applies in our everyday, nonwork circumstances. For him, it is summed up in one principle, the Golden Rule: "Do unto others as you would have them do unto you." If you follow that, your behavior will be ethical; if you depart from it, it won't be. At work or at home, in the office or in the neighborhood, it's the same.

The Golden Rule and its variants ("Don't treat others differently than you would want to be treated," "If something is disagreeable to you, don't treat others that way," etc.) are common to many ethical and religious traditions. If there were one single candidate for a common ethical principle among all the various cultures, it would no doubt be this one. Whether it is the *only* ethical principle is another question. But, be that as it may, Maxwell is surely correct on the point that ethics in the context of business is simply an extension of ethics in general. There aren't special exceptions for business. It's as wrong to lie to your competitor as it is to lie to your neighbor.

All of us, of course, have encountered different attitudes. We have heard "But this is business" said as if it meant "Anything goes." Certainly, some people feel that way. People who would never cheat in a neighborhood card game can be perfectly content to deceive their

---

[2] Maxwell, John. *There's No Such Thing as Business Ethics.* New York: Warner Books, 2003.

customers or rip off their suppliers. But this doesn't show that such people are operating according to a special "business ethic"; rather, it simply reveals that, in this context, they have made the decision to be unethical.

Whether in the business, professional, or even political context, when we speak of people of integrity we are speaking of those who bring to their job or office the same standards that apply in personal life. Telling the truth, keeping your word, treating others with decency and respect—these are traits that we expect of people personally (that is, these are standards to which people are held), and those who adhere to these standards in their professional lives as well are the ones who we say have integrity.

I absolutely agree with Maxwell that ethics in business is really no different than ethics in everyday life. This goes for the real estate business as much as any other kind of business. On the other hand, though, professional ethics can seem a lot more complicated. There are all those rules! And the rules—especially when we're considering something like the Realtor® Code of Ethics—can sometimes seem pretty esoteric. That's a topic to which we shall now turn.

Code of Ethics of the National Association of Realtors®

The National Association of Realtors® (NAR) is rightfully proud of its *Code of Ethics*, a document first formulated in 1913 and amended at 31 different national conventions since then. The 17 articles of the Code are supplemented by 73 *Standards of Practice*, which supply more specific applications of the articles. Moreover, an official part of the Code is the *Interpretations of the Code of Ethics*. This collection currently consists of 142 Case Interpretations, each of which is designed to show how the underlying article applies to a specific set of circumstances.[3]

---

[3] Those numbers were current at the time this was being written in 2006. They change almost every year as new Standards of Practice and Case Interpretations are added.

Now, no one, I think, has all this stuff memorized, though there are probably plenty of people who know the basic articles by heart.

The fact that the Code is continually being amended, modified, and updated is a good thing. It shows that the Code of Ethics is a living document, adaptable to ever-changing business and technological environments. Don't get me wrong. It is not that the principles of the Code change as business practices change. To the contrary. The principles remain the same, but updates and occasionally restatements are needed in order to show how those unchanging principles apply in new situations—situations that couldn't even have been imagined ten, twenty, and thirty years earlier.

The NAR Code of Ethics is not a unique phenomenon. There are hundreds of professional and trade group codes of ethics. Physicians, lawyers, funeral directors, and wedding planners—to name just a few— all have professional codes of ethics. So also do many individual companies and corporations. They vary, of course, in range and complexity.

If it is true that business ethics in general, and those of the real estate profession in particular, are all simply extensions of the ethical principles of everyday life, then it is reasonable to ask: Why are there so many professional codes and provisions? Why are they necessary? How is it that they can become so complicated?

Professional codes of ethics serve essentially four purposes, although not every code serves all four.

(1) *Codes of ethics bring to our attention and provide direction with respect to issues that might not otherwise even have been identified as matters of ethical concern.*

For example: The Realtor® Code of Ethics requires that any advertisement of a listed property for sale must include the professional status of the Realtor® doing the advertising and the name of the Realtor® firm. What, one might ask, is the ethical concern here? The answer is: Without such identification a potential buyer might be wrongfully misled to think that the property was being advertised by the owner.

Now, that might not have occurred to one of us, unaided. The Code, as it were, brings to our attention the fact that there is a chance for misleading here, and that is something we want to avoid.

(2) *In many situations, codes of ethics provide us with the wisdom and insight of those who have preceded us.*

This is not to say that we are to look to the limits and directions of professional codes as if they were holy writ, to be followed without question. Rather, it is to note that we are well served by paying attention to the thoughts of those who have faced situations similar to the ones we face and who have thought them through on the basis of principles with which we all agree. There is, after all, no special merit in constantly reinventing the wheel.

Standard of Practice 3-4 of the Realtor® Code of Ethics states that Realtors® have "an affirmative obligation to disclose the existence of dual or variable rate commission arrangements" to potential cooperating brokers and to disclose to those brokers, upon inquiry, what the differential would be. (A dual or variable rate commission is one where a different commission is payable if the listing broker procures the buyer—that is, the deal is "double-ended"—rather than if a cooperating broker brings the buyer.)

Suppose that you have a listing with a variable rate commission such that the seller pays 5% if the buyer is brought by another broker, but 4% if you bring the buyer yourself. If another broker asked you what the difference would be between an in-house and a coop sale, Standard of Practice 3-4 would require you to tell him or her.

Now, in the absence of that Standard of Practice, you might not be inclined to tell the other broker. Even though you know generally that you have a duty to cooperate with other brokers, you might think that revealing the nature of the variable rate commission goes beyond cooperation. Your reaction might be that it's just not the other broker's business.

However, if you sat down and thought about it a lot, you might come to see that sharing the information is really in the interest of your client, that it is a natural extension of the duty to cooperate, and that the requirement to do so can be traced back to the Golden Rule. But, in the hustle and bustle of everyday life and transactions, neither you nor I would sit down and think such things through. That's why it is useful to have a code there to help us.

(3) *Professional ethics codes sometimes also cover matters that are not so much ethical as they are issues of professional etiquette or proper procedure.*

The Code of Ethics of the American Institute of Architects, for example, includes a provision that members "should recognize and give credit to others for the professional work they have performed." (Canon V, E.5.5.2) Few would see this as, strictly speaking, an ethical issue. It's a matter of etiquette.

In the Realtor® Code of Ethics, Article 17 deals with the obligations of Realtors® to submit procuring cause disputes to "arbitration in accordance with the regulations of their Board or Boards...." Again, this is a provision that does not deal with what most of us would think is a specifically ethical issue. It is, rather, a procedural one within the profession.

(4) *Professional ethics codes are also sometimes used for the purposes of "drawing lines" in order to remove any unclarity about what may be considered acceptable or unacceptable.*

For example, there are companies and legislative bodies whose ethics codes specify that employees or members cannot accept a gift above a certain value, say $75 or $100. As of July 2005, members of Congress could not, except in specified circumstances, accept gifts with a value of more than $50 and a yearly aggregate value (from any one source) of more than $100. Certainly, one could argue that $75 and a $125 aggregate might be just as acceptable. And that might well be. But the point of limits like these is not to get things exactly ethically right (if that idea even makes sense), but simply to draw a line—if anything, erring on the side of caution—for the sake of clarity.

The point of these comments is twofold. (1) It is to note that the Realtor® Code of Ethics is not some unique phenomenon, standing out there all on its own. Rather, it is well within a substantial tradition of ethics codes that are to be found in literally thousands of companies and professional associations. (2) It is to emphasize that, while professional and organizational codes may have a variety of purposes, and while they may sometimes have what seem to us to be oddly specific provisions, all of them are grounded in what we might call "the ethics of everyday life."

Different codes may call for what, on the surface, might appear to be very different kinds of behavior. For example, the ethics code of the American Association of Pastoral Counselors (as amended in 1994) prohibits the use of client testimonials in advertising. No such prohibition exists in the Realtor® Code, and as a matter of fact, most real estate professionals would agree that client testimonials are a significant and positive aspect of real estate advertising. Does this show that professional ethics codes are somehow arbitrary and/or removed from a common ethical base? Not at all. Rather, it shows how the applications of the *same* principles, such as the Golden Rule, may yield different results in different situations.

Ethics and the Law

The relationship between the law and ethics in general is not an altogether clear one, so it is no surprise that, for Realtors®, it is sometimes confusing that the requirements of the Code of Ethics and of the law may differ.

First of all, we need to note that, although many of our everyday ethical norms are found in the law also, this means neither that our ethics are derived from the law nor that what is found in the law is necessarily the same as what ethics would tell us.

Laws can be "antiquated" and can prohibit behavior that we may find ethically and morally acceptable (although the behavior may have been considered unacceptable at the time the laws were passed). Some states still have blue laws, which prohibit various commercial activities on Sunday, and almost every state has laws on the books that seem just plain silly. Web sites such as *dumblaw.com* are full of them.

Conversely, the law may allow all sorts of behavior that may not be ethically acceptable. Except for certain specific circumstances, there are no laws against lying or treating people in a mean and degrading manner. Yet, by applying the Golden Rule, we know that such behavior is not ethically acceptable.

When it comes to the relationship between the law and the Realtor® Code of Ethics, what we find is that the Code of Ethics may often demand of us more than the law requires.

One simple example: Article 4 of the Code of Ethics requires that a Realtor® disclose to a seller if the Realtor® is related to the buyer. In California, though, the law requires only that you, as an agent, make such a disclosure to a *buyer* when you are related to the seller. California law does not require, as the Code does, that you make a similar disclosure to a seller if you happen to be related to the buyer.[4] In that situation, then, the Code requires more of us than does the law.

Realtors® should also be aware that, in some jurisdictions, they may find themselves held legally accountable to the standards spelled out in the Code. In 2005 the Risk Management Committee of the National Association of Realtors® (NAR) released a letter warning state and local associations that "By adopting standards, even if identified as 'voluntary,' the standards can be claimed to represent the legal standards by which the legal liability of all brokers is measured." The context of the NAR letter concerned standards proposed by the Real Estate Standards Institute, most of which ranged from matters of common courtesy to simple good business practices. The point, though, remains the same.

The NAR letter referred to a long history of court reliance on standards of practice established through the Realtor® Code of Ethics. Now, the Code of Ethics is not law. It is voluntarily adopted by those who are members of a particular trade association. Nonetheless, courts have held that these standards may set the bar of liability, applying

---

[4] I'm not saying that California law makes sense. I am just pointing out that it differs from the Code of Ethics on this issue.

even to nonmembers. As the Arizona Supreme Court quaintly put it in 1962, the NAR Code of Ethics "is regarded as the standard of conduct by real estate men throughout the United States and shall be regarded as such in the State of Arizona."

When we are uneasy about the right course of action in some situation, it is always a good idea to determine what, if anything, the law has to say. But simply finding out that something is not prohibited by the law does not tell us that, from an ethical point of view, it is therefore OK to do it. "Is it legal?" is always a good question to ask; and we want the answer to be "Yes." But there is a next question too. The next question should be "Is it right?"

Fiduciary Duty: The Requirements of Agency

One aspect of the ethical duties of real estate agents falls out of the norm of everyday ethics. This is to be found in the notion of *fiduciary duties*. Being a fiduciary isn't something that conflicts with common ethics, but it is a relationship that represents the exception rather than the typical.

The pages of this book are hardly the place for a legal treatise on the concept of fiduciary duty. Nor would I be capable of presenting such a treatise. Suffice it here to note what the Realtor® Code of Ethics says: "When representing a buyer, seller, landlord, tenant, or other client as an agent, Realtors® pledge themselves to protect and promote the interests of their client. This obligation to the client is primary...."

Let us contrast this with our normal or typical relationships with others. That is, if we are to conduct ourselves ethically, it is important that we take into consideration the thoughts, feelings, and welfare of others. We must take into account how our actions will affect others, sometimes even other people who are not known to us.

Taking others into account goes to the bedrock of ethical conduct, namely, the notion that everyone counts. Taking others into account is the behavioral embodiment of the Golden Rule. It is the habit of "putting ourselves into the other person's shoes." It is asking, "Would I want this done to me?" It acknowledges our basic equality. It is central to ethical living.

But taking others into account does *not* mean that we must promote their interests above our own. Ethics in general does not require self-denial, and ethical behavior is not measured by the degree to which we become a doormat. There is nothing inherently unethical about living and conducting our business in a way that enhances our own self interest. Ethics simply requires that we do not advance our own self-interest by breaking rules, ignoring duties, or acting with disregard for the well-being of others.

Having said that, though, we also need to acknowledge that we can and do put ourselves into relationships such that we may subordinate our own self-interest to that of someone else. When we make a promise, we create a duty to do something. If I promise to lend you my car tomorrow, then I have a duty to you to make the car available. I don't have any duty to others to make my car available to them (unless I've made similar promises). Later, it may turn out that keeping the promise is burdensome, but the duty is still there.

So, yes, ethics generally does *not* require us to put the interests of others ahead of our own. But there can be special circumstances and special relationships—which we ourselves may have created or entered into—such that our own interests become secondary to those of another.

This is what happens when, as Realtors®, we take on the role of agents. In that situation, it is our duty to promote the interest of another, and, if our interests conflict, theirs must prevail.

Some people get into the real estate business without thinking about the ethical obligations of agency (legal ones, too), and when they hear of it, they chafe. Indeed, some agents' behavior would lead you to think that they are the *adversaries* of those who are supposed to be their clients. They just want to get as much out of them as they can, and they really don't care about how the client does.

Not only does that kind of self-interested attitude fly in the face of the ethical obligations created by a fiduciary relationship, but also it is usually counterproductive. Real estate, done well, is a repeat and referral business, and the way to get that kind of business is to put your clients' interests first. Ironically, it serves your own self-interest—in the long run—to do so. There is truth to the adage "The more you help others get what they want, the more you will get what you want."

Why Do the Right Thing?

The last section ended with the notion that at least one aspect of ethical behavior—helping others get what they want—may actually work to serve our own self-interest. While I believe that is true, I certainly couldn't *prove* it. The evidence is, at best, anecdotal. There are no comprehensive studies to cite or controlled experiments we can refer to. Moreover, one would be reluctant to try to put the point in terms of specific financial rewards.

There are two extreme positions—myths, if you will—that ought to be avoided. One is that ethical living will inevitably be good for you financially. The other is that ethical living will inevitably be bad for you financially. Neither is correct. While we all have lots of stories, experiences, and perspectives, no one has anything like proof or conclusive evidence to support such extreme views.

Well, if not the extremes, what about the tendencies? Are you at least more likely to be financially successful if you live ethically, or is it more likely that unethical behavior will hurt you financially? Again, there's no conclusive proof here, but recently, some interesting studies have been conducted.

Thomas Kostigen of *MarketWatch* relates a Penn State study that showed how reputable companies had gained financially. Between 1983 and 1997, Fortune's most-admired companies increased annual returns, on average, by 22%. James Mitchell, author of *The Ethical Advantage*, refers to a Harvard Business School study that showed differences between companies that had an ethical culture and those that didn't. Over an eleven-year period, the former experienced revenue growth four times as fast, and stock price increases 12 times as great, as the latter. Other studies have shown that companies have better employee-retention rates when the employees perceive their bosses to be persons of integrity.

Again, these kinds of studies don't provide conclusive proof that ethical business practices will be more profitable than nonethical ones, but they are certainly relevant for consideration.

Doing the right thing and practicing business in an ethical manner is definitely not incompatible with financial success, and well might even enhance it. But that's not the *reason* to live that way. We live that way because we value ourselves.

To honor someone is to hold them in esteem or respect. When we honor a person we ascribe worth of some sort to them. We may honor someone, or give them honors, for their athletic prowess, achievements, bravery, or even sales skills. But how does this relate to one's *personal* honor, the kind of honor we mean when we say, "on my honor"?

As the act of honoring another is to ascribe worth to them, the person who *has* honor ascribes worth to himself. (Conversely, I believe, the person who lacks a sense of honor is a person who lacks self-worth.) It is a worth based on character, not skills. Honor is not equivalent to integrity, but it derives from it. A person who has honor, or a sense of honor, is a person who lives by a code and/or a set of principles, and who finds such value in doing so that he or she counts it as a basis of worth.

One of Tom Clancy's characters relays the thought that honor is "a man's gift to himself." Although putting it this way may not be politically correct, the notion is a sound one. Whether we live with honor or not is up to us. No one can give us honor but ourselves, and no one else can take it away.

Doing the right thing, living with honor, choosing the ethical alternative, is often referred to as "taking the high road." Why take the high road? Not because it is the way to financial success, though it might be. It is the road to be taken not for where it leads, but just for what it means to be on it. Besides, the air is cleaner, the view is better, and it is a whole lot less crowded.

2

Prospecting

Prospecting is where it all begins. As Gary Keller, founder of Keller Williams Realty, puts it, "Nothing is more important to your sales career than prospective buyers and sellers. To have a viable business, you simply must have client leads."

Where are such leads to come from? Prospecting.

As we use the terms here, and certainly others might use them differently, *prospecting* and *advertising* are not the same. Certainly, there may be some overlap. Moreover, it is not important that we have a precise distinction, as long as you get the idea. When we advertise, we are usually trying to sell (or lease) a particular piece of property. Prospecting, on the other hand, is an activity that is designed to bring us new clients, new leads.

Thus we may have an overlap when we do what we call "institutional" or promotional advertising, which is designed to attract people to our business, our brand if you wish, not necessarily to buy a particular property. Conversely, we may obtain new clientele as a result of advertising that is designed to sell a certain property. It happens.

All sorts of activities may fall within the category of prospecting. It can be anything from door knocking to playing golf regularly at the club. Some prospecting activities can be quite enjoyable; others may be sheer misery. It depends on the person, not the activity. Regardless of whether it is enjoyable or not, the first goal of prospecting is to let people know that you are in the real estate business. This doesn't necessarily confine your prospecting to people you don't know. It is distressing and astounding to learn how many people whom you do know don't know that you are in the real estate business. They may have forgotten, or they may have assumed—not having heard from you—that you, like so many others, have dropped out.

But there is a second, more important goal. That is, you want to give those people a reason to use your services or to refer you to someone. Unless you live in a very unusual place, the people you contact already know at least one other real estate agent, maybe dozens. In your prospecting activity, then, you need to differentiate yourself.

It is in doing that differentiating that we are likely to run into ethical issues. As we try, however subtly, to convince others that we are the right ones to choose for real estate services, it is tempting, ever so tempting, to make ourselves look a little better than we actually are or to portray ourselves in a misleading way. That is one of the things we need to watch out for.

Misleading Metatags

Frances and Bill had been friends for years—friends through thick and thin, including the death of Frances' husband and Bill's lifelong buddy, Eric. It was not unusual, then, for them to be having lunch together. What *was* unusual was the item that Bill handed to her following their traditional toast and sip of a mutually favorite Syrah. The item: a $5,000 check. "Bill, what is this about?" she asked in an incredulous tone.

"Fran," he responded, "this is really just a small token of my appreciation to you. You have no idea of the impact you have had on my business. I know it was nothing you intended, or even thought about, but because of you, I have radically altered my business model, and I am now making amounts of money—without hardly working at all!—that I never even dreamed about."

"What ...," she began; but he cut her off before she could even formulate the question. "Remember, four years ago, not long after Eric's death, when you made the decision to move out of this valley, up to the mountain, and to maintain only a low-key business occasionally selling vacation homes?" Of course, she did. "You asked me if I could send you any referrals that came my way—people who might have come through the valley, or come in contact with me some other way, but who wanted to own something up on the hill, a little ski chalet or some such thing."

Frances nodded, "And you sent me quite a few."

"I don't think I ever shared with you the details of this, Fran, but almost all of those referrals came from my Internet site." Frances looked puzzled. "Look," Bill continued, "I don't even know exactly how all this stuff works, but my web page guy does. What happened was that I told him about wanting to be able to send referrals to you. So, what he did—and again, don't ask me details—was to add to my web site a page, actually a number of pages, about the mountain. I mean, it was like he did a chamber of commerce thing. It had something to do with what he called *metatags* too. He fixed it all up so that if someone went on the Internet and tried to find out about skiing on the mountain, or real estate on the mountain, they were pretty likely to wind up on my web site. Then, if they indicated any interest, I would just give them your name as a "best Realtor®" and have you contact them. That's where all those referrals came from that I have been sending you."

"Wow" was about as much as Fran could exclaim. "I wondered where they all came from. And it's been great. But what does that have to do with this check?"

"Fran, what I did with you out of friendship struck me as something I could do with others for money. I mean, I never could have done it without the web guy, but it has just been a gold mine."

"What?"

"Well, what I do—what *he* does would be more accurate—is to set up all these web pages that make it look like they are *the* real estate site to go to for Palm Springs, Hilton Head, Maui, Stowe, Aspen—you name it. People get sucked into my web pages for all these different places—all vacation spots—thinking that I am the guy or the institution to go to if they want to find out about these places. Then, when they express an interest in real estate, I set them up with a referral in the area. The local agent finds them a place, everyone is happy, and I collect a 25%

referral fee. I do practically no work—certainly no real estate work—and I'm making five times what I was schlepping houses here in the valley.

"And, Fran, I owe it all to you."

"Bill, I am so happy for you. And for me too," she said, lightly waving the check in the air with one hand, while raising her glass in the other. "To our continued success!"

Misleading Metatags: Comments and Analysis

First, a word about metatags. According to *Wikipedia*, "Meta elements provide information about a given webpage, most often to help search engines categorize them correctly." Metatags are words that certain kinds of Internet search engines use to identify what a given web page is about. Thus, if someone wanted a search engine to find their page when the searcher was looking for web pages about Palm Springs, the expression *Palm Springs* might be included as a metatag, even though Palm Springs did not appear on the title of the web page. *The key here is that metatags are not seen by the individual who is looking.* Rather, they are "seen" by the search engine (such as Google's, or Yahoo's), and the search engine then turns up the page as one that the person might be interested in. Metatags are not now—in 2007—nearly as important to searches as they were in the 1990s, but they still operate in basically the same way.

Suppose that someone challenged what Bill was doing as being unethical. Bill might defend himself by saying two things: (1) He might say that he hadn't *lied* to anyone. His web sites didn't actually claim to be *from* Miami Beach, Steamboat Springs, or wherever; they just provided a lot of information *about* those places. (2) Besides, what if visitors to the sites did make those assumptions? So what? It was all good information, and no one was harmed. They got what they wanted. So where's the wrong in that?

With respect to (1), let us note that this is a classic defense to the charge that you have misled someone. Sometimes it's called "lawyering," but it's hardly something anyone has to go to law school to learn. Little kids do it almost intuitively—"I didn't hit him, Mom!" (Of course, I *did* pinch him ...) But the problem is not lying; the problem is misleading someone.

Article 12 of the Realtor® Code of Ethics says, "Realtors® shall be careful at all times to present a true picture in their advertising and representations to the public." A "true picture" here doesn't just mean one that lacks false information. It means a picture or representation that conveys relevant information and that does nothing to lead an observer down a path toward false information or mistaken inferences. This is a good example of the Golden Rule underlying the Code. We don't want to be treated in such a way. We tend to resent it when a person or an institution tries to mislead us. Hence, we should not try to mislead others.

The second defense—that no one was harmed—merits two distinct responses.

First of all, *even if* no one was harmed, it is still generally wrong to mislead people. Ethical assessments—even overarching ethical viewpoints—frequently differ depending on whether we focus on *outcomes* or whether we put our emphasis on general moral rules. This is not the place to engage in a wide-ranging debate on the matter. But we can note a couple of items.

Actions can be wrong, even if they don't have bad outcomes. Suppose, for example, that I deliberately failed to disclose to a buyer of my house my knowledge that the attic furnace is defective and that it could easily cause a fire. Now, even if the buyer, on his own initiative, decided to replace the furnace, and no harm ever came from my failure to disclose, it still would have been wrong of me not to have told him.

Conversely, there can be situations when doing something that is generally wrong to do might, because of the circumstances, be the ethically correct thing. If a woman had asked you for protection from an agitated and intoxicated abusive husband, it would certainly be ethically acceptable for you to tell him falsely that you didn't know where she could be found.

But situations where "breaking the rules" are the right thing to do are rare, indeed. Almost always, they will involve preventing harm. But that's not the kind of situation Bill was in. His deception wasn't preventing harm for the sake of some greater good; he was just serving his own self-interest. And that's not enough to justify breaking the rules.

The second response to the "no one was harmed" defense is to question whether that is really correct. It is not unusual for people to justify questionable behavior by claiming that no one was harmed. Frequently, though, the only reason that this claim seems plausible is that we have not, so to speak, cast the net wide enough in our consideration of who might have been affected.

The term *stakeholders* is used frequently in business ethics. To be sure, it is a play on *stockholders,* and it refers to every one who has a stake in— who might be affected by—a particular action or decision. Thus, when a large company decides to close a plant in a town where it is a major employer, the stakeholders are not just the employees and the company's stockholders. Stakeholders would include local suppliers and vendors, nearby merchants, even the school district.

When Bill says that "no one was harmed" by his Internet program, probably he was not considering all the stakeholders who were affected by his actions. Quite likely there were legitimate local agents who lost out on business—business that they otherwise might have had—because of Bill's web site. It's a pretty sure thing that they would say they had been harmed.

Interested readers might want to take a look at the Realtor® Code of Ethics Case Interpretation 12-17. That study involves the use of another company's name, which would be pretty unusual, but the point is the same. Nowadays, probably the most common domain name, keyword, or metatag offense with respect to misleading concerns the use of the term MLS.

In any event, NAR has recently adopted Standard of Practice 12-10, which, among other things, prohibits:

> ... deceptively using metatags, keywords or other devices/methods to direct, drive, or divert Internet traffic, or to otherwise mislead consumers.

This will help prevent people from being misled as to who it is they are dealing with. It will help to ensure that a true picture is presented. This is but one example of how the Code continually needs amending in order to stay current with new technologies.

"Solds"

There were a lot of reasons that Gail and Maria had decided to come to work for Dan. Although his company didn't have a well-known franchise name, he had plenty of market share in the town. And Dan would be the first to acknowledge that his company's success was a result of the fact that his agents were happy. Not that they were happy-happy, full of fun and grins. Rather, they were happy because of the way Dan ran his business. He, himself, was as innovative as any marketing guru in the biggest of the big companies. He was always conducting promotions, running ad campaigns, and coming up with marketing schemes that kept the community paying attention and his agents doing business.

Also, and this may have been even more important, he was extremely supportive of his agents, giving them plenty of rein to do business and advertise themselves as they saw fit. Not that Dan would tolerate anything illegal or unethical. "Always tell the truth," he told his agents, loosely quoting Mark Twain, "it will gratify your friends and confound your enemies."

So there they were—Gail and Maria—wet behind the ears, full of enthusiasm, and ready to conquer the real estate world in the name of Dan's company, The Best Realty Company. Just one question remained: Where to start?

"I think you two could just knock them dead in the Highlands tract," Dan said at their second business plan meeting. "It's—what?—four to five years old now, and while there have been resales all along, no big numbers. But, now should be about the time for a lot of those folks to be putting their homes on the market. That was a first-time buyer tract, young marrieds by and large, with no kids or maybe just one. Now they have two or three, and they are ready to move up. I tell you, it's going to take off as a listing farm.

"Not only that, but no one dominates in there. The sales that have occurred have been by an agent here, an agent there—all over the board. I don't think any one agent has even three sales in that tract.

"Trust me; if you put your efforts in the Highlands tract, your careers are going into zoom mode really fast. Work hard, be innovative, and you'll never regret it."

Dan was a great motivator, and Gail and Maria were really pumped. They hit the ground running. They mailed, they walked, and they knocked. They provided "garage sale" signs, and they sponsored a Little League team. Some weeks, it seemed, they spent more time in the neighborhood than anyone who lived in the neighborhood. But then a cold, hard reality set in. In three different conversations they heard essentially the same message: "You are wonderful, enthusiastic girls [why did people have to call them "girls"?!], but when we list, I think we want to be with someone who has had some more experience."

It was the day after the third time they had heard this refrain, when "the girls" were having a glass of wine together, that Maria had her idea. "Look," she said, "we're not going to lie or anything, but let's do something to give the impression we have had the kind of experience people want us to have."

Her idea was simple and straightforward. In their next newsletter they would include a map of the area. At the location of each home that had sold in the past couple of years, there would be a "Sold" indicated. About half, certainly not all, of the "Solds" would appear in the distinctive **SOLD** lettering used by Dan's company. Each of those would be accompanied by an asterisk, leading to the notation "And we can sell yours too!"

Why some, but not all of them? "Look, Gail, no one would believe that we or our company sold *all* the homes in the tract; but they very well might believe that we sold a lot of them.

"The beauty of this is that we are not saying anything that isn't true. If some people infer that the "Solds" marked by the special lettering were in fact sold by our company—or by us—well, that's their doing. 'And we can sell yours too!' certainly doesn't say or claim that we were the ones who sold those properties. It just says what it says."

Maria was right, of course: quite a few people did make the inference, without Maria or Gail saying anything. To be sure, they had to dance around some questions, but because they really had done their homework on the comps, they were able to answer questions about price, condition, and market time without ever actually claiming to have been the listing agents.

In time, and after a few more issues of the newsletter, the idea paid off. First one listing, then another, and then another. The Highlands tract took off as a resale area, and Gail's and Maria's careers took off with it. Dan was right; they never regretted it.

"Solds": Comments and Analysis

The core ethical issue here is the same as that in the first case, *Metatags*. The problem is misleading people, and, as we have observed earlier, it is the most likely ethical issue to arise in the area of prospecting. When we are prospecting, we not only want people to know we are Realtors®, we also want to give them a reason to consider using our services rather than those of a competitor. When we need to differentiate ourselves from the others, the temptation can be great to try to portray ourselves as having qualities or experiences that we may not actually have. It is a temptation to present something other than a "true picture," and it is an especially luring temptation to those who are new in the business and don't yet have a track record to put on display.

It's easy to get confused about the rules governing the use of saying "sold," though when we examine them we can see the sense of the rules, and we can feel comfortable about following them.

The first rule to note is that the listing broker is not the only one who is permitted to say that he or she sold a particular property. The cooperating broker (there's a reason they call them *the selling agent*) may also make that claim. Standard of Practice 12-7 says:

> Only Realtors® who participated in the transaction as the listing broker or cooperating broker (selling broker) may claim to have "sold" the property. Prior to closing, a cooperating broker may post a "sold" sign only with the consent of the listing broker.

Two comments:

(1) It is certainly reasonable and consistent with the intent of the "true picture" principle that only these two (listing broker and cooperating broker) can make the claim. Many years ago, a friend of mine (a good, creative, person) who was new to the area—i.e., without a local track record—ran ads that said things like "We did it again! The property on 125 Main Street was sold through our MLS!" His defense, rightfully unsuccessful, was that it was true that the property sold through MLS. But his ad misled people to think that his office had something to do with it.

(2) Certainly, within the Code, a balancing of interests is going on. Many Code provisions are designed to keep consumers from being misled or confused; yet certainly there is potential for confusion when two different Realtors® (the listing agent and the selling agent) can send out postcards saying "I sold the house at 32 Elm Street!" On the other hand, though, it seems entirely appropriate to let the cooperating broker (*the selling agent*) make that claim as much as the listing broker.

The other possible source of confusion has to do with newsletters and the publication of factual material. It is OK within the Code of Ethics to send out a newsletter that publishes factual material derived from the MLS. But you have to be careful here. Suppose you sent out a letter that included the following, and only the following, about neighborhood market activity:

It's Been a Busy Month!

<u>Just Listed</u>

| 2605 Mariner's Way $595,000 | 3 bdr., 2.5 bath, Sea Captain Model |
| 1879 Seafarer $639,000 | 4 bdr., 3 bath, Commodore Model |

<u>Pending Sale</u>

| 2406 Captain's Watch $615,000 list | 4 bdr., 3 bath, Commodore Model |

<u>Closed Sales</u>

| 1855 Main Sail $565,000 | 2 bdr., 2 bath, Windjammer Model |
| 2918 Safe Harbor $645,000 | 5 bdr., 3 bath, Admiral Model |

If nothing else were said, it could be argued that you intended for readers to think that all of this represented your own personal activity, *your* busy month.. If you are going to send out news of this sort, and it includes news about the work product of others, then you really need to include some sort of disclaimer and indication that this is from MLS, that it includes activity from other companies, etc. Good guidance on this can be gleaned from the Realtor® Code of Ethics Case Interpretations 12-12 and 12-13.

In the case of Gail and Maria, their "news" was designed to mislead. Was anyone harmed by that? Maybe, maybe not; but, as we have seen, that doesn't decide the issue. Even if no one was hurt by their act of misleading, it was something they shouldn't have done. And they didn't need to be old-timer ethics pros to know that. The Golden Rule would have told them.

Referrals

Carl really couldn't see any harm in talking to Josh about his "secrets of success." After all, Josh, his nephew, lived thousands of miles away, and nothing that he was going to do in his budding real estate career could possibly have an impact on Carl's business. Who knows? If Josh stuck with it and became successful, he might even send Carl referrals some day, or vice versa.

It wasn't just an idle issue for Carl. He'd had many opportunities to tell people how he worked. His broker, the franchise regional director, and even the bigwigs back at franchise headquarters had been trying for years to get him to speak at one of their annual, semiannual, quarterly, or whatever meetings. He always refused. His excuse to them was a fear of speaking in public and stuff like that. But it wasn't the real reason. The real reason was that he was always concerned that someone at one of those meetings would be from his market area and would take his very successful methods back home and use them in competition against him. It'd be better that he just keep quiet about his methods of attracting business.

So when Josh came to Uncle Carl at the family reunion and asked if Carl would set aside some time to talk to him about the business and how he had become so successful, Carl was obliging. Not only was Carl flattered, but he was also delighted with Josh's enthusiasm, which was still at a pretty high level for a licensee of just six months. Josh had already closed a couple of deals, so he knew he could do it; but where and how, he wanted to know, could he build a business like that of Uncle Carl?

"You're a bright kid, Josh, and I'm sure you've already picked up on the fact that this is a referral business. Did you know that a NAR survey showed 43% of sellers and 44% of buyers used an agent who was referred to them? That's a pretty big slice of the pie, Son. And when you add to it that another 28% of the sellers and 11% of buyers used an agent they had previously worked with, well, there aren't a whole lot of people left for the other sources of business—like signs, newspaper ads, and Internet sites."

Josh had not heard those numbers before, and as he turned them over in his mind, he could see that they had really big implications.

"I bet I know what you are thinking, Josh. If so much depends on referrals and past business, how does a new guy ever make it? Well, let me tell you two things. One, it isn't easy. But, two, it sure isn't impossible either, especially if you work smart."

"That's what I'm here for, Uncle Carl. Tell me about working smart."

"Well, Josh, I figured out a long time ago that one of the main reasons so many agents flounder is that—even though they know that real estate is a referral business—they don't work their referrals like a business. They may be great at listing and selling, getting the financing, and jumping through all the legal hoops, but they're really pretty poor at securing referrals. And that's what they need to do.

"Oh, some agents—but not very many, I'll tell you—are good about keeping in touch with past clients, and most people who farm neighborhoods have learned to ask now and then if the person they are talking to knows anyone who wants to buy or sell. But usually this is done in kind of a half-baked way, and there's hardly ever anything businesslike about it.

"So, here's the problem with most agents, Josh, and I don't want it to be a problem for you. Most of them don't cast their nets wide enough; they rely on only one or two sources—maybe their farm, or social network, or former clients—for referrals; and they don't have anything that resembles a business plan for obtaining referrals from those they do contact.

"Let me tell you what I do.

"First of all, I cast the net wide. Sure, I let my friends and past clients know that I want referral business. But I also get the word out to the mail deliverers, pool service guys, termite inspectors, painters, and carpet cleaners—to name the main ones—anyone who is liable to talk with homeowners, and especially those whom owners might be contacting if they are getting ready to sell.

"For buyer referrals it's a little harder to target, because you don't know where they are coming from or who their city contacts are liable to be. I'll tell you some, though: people who work in the school district offices, of course, personnel people at any large local companies, and the folks who work at the chamber of commerce. You have to be a little careful about the chamber of commerce thing, because a lot of other real estate agents belong. But you can work it out to do some things on the Q.T.

"Now, these people that you want to be referral sources, you need to let them know that this is business. None of these "I ♥ referrals" stickers or something with a smiley face. You give them a business proposition.

"I offer my referral sources 20% of the commission I receive when the deal closes, and I have a little form made up that I'll sign. It's just a version of one of those franchise real estate referral forms, but, again, it lets them know it's a business deal.

"Most of these people have heard referral pitches from real estate agents before, but not with numbers like I offer. Other people say, 'I'll give you a hundred dollars' or 'I'll buy you dinner' somewhere. Not me. This is serious. I even give my referral sources a couple of scripts they can use when they refer me. I've taught them that they increase the chances that the seller or buyer will call me if they can say something about my credentials and experience as opposed to just 'There's this real estate agent I know.'

"And you had better believe they want to increase the chances, with the kind of referral fees I offer!

"Are you thinking it sounds expensive? Let me put it this way: There's not an agent I know who wouldn't pay a 20% referral fee—nowadays they are more like 25% and 30%—to another real estate agent for a referral. So why shouldn't I pay 20% to a civilian? I'll do that all day long. Besides, I don't have to pay $500 to $1,000 to join some referral network and advertise in their publication.

"Real estate is a referral business, Josh, so work your referral sources like a business. You'll do great, and I'll bet your competitors will never figure it out. Just don't tell them, OK? You don't want to get into bidding wars over your local contacts.

"Now, there are lots more details I could be giving you, but first, do you have any questions?"

Referrals: Comments and Analysis

What can we say about Carl? He's aggressive, maybe a touch arrogant, but he does seem to know what he's doing—and what his competition isn't doing. He knows that you constantly have to keep trying to attract new business, and he knows that referrals are the absolute golden way to do that. So, is there a problem here? Is he doing anything ethically wrong? I would say so, because Carl is involved in clear violations of regulations under RESPA.

RESPA—the Real Estate Settlement and Procedures Act—was enacted by Congress in 1974 as consumer-protection legislation. Among its provisions, RESPA generally prohibits practices such as the payment of kickbacks and almost all referral fees. These are prohibited, because the authors of RESPA believed that such practices resulted in increased costs paid by consumers.

The main exception to RESPA's anti-kickback provisions is that it does allow for referral fees to be paid between real estate brokers. A Realtor® in Virginia may refer a client to a Realtor® in Wyoming and be paid a referral fee for doing so. This is allowed under RESPA. RESPA does not, however, allow for referral fees to be paid by a real estate broker (or agent) to an unlicensed person.[5] You cannot pay a referral fee to your brother-in-law if he does not have a real estate license. Of course, you might not have wanted to pay him a referral fee anyway, but that is another issue.

There are a couple of factors about RESPA and referral fees that may lead to some confusion. One is that RESPA is federal law, and, in some cases, it may not align with state law. In California, for example, real estate law does *not* prohibit the payment of referral fees to unlicensed persons. So, a licensee in California could pay a referral fee to the (unlicensed) postman and have nothing to worry about as far as the California Department of Real Estate is concerned. But that licensee *does* have to worry about the Department of Housing and Urban Development (HUD), which is the organization that enforces the federal RESPA law.

A second, sometimes confusing, aspect of RESPA is that it applies only to a certain class of transactions. RESPA applies to a residential property transaction (up to four units) in which "federally related" financing is used. Financing by a lender whose deposits or accounts are federally insured would be covered, as would loans that are, or are intended to be, sold to secondary market institutions such as Fannie Mae or Freddie Mac. RESPA does not cover commercial transactions, nor does it apply to transactions that involve only cash and/or seller financing.

Having said that, we simply note that RESPA applies to an overwhelming majority of the transactions that most agents are involved in: residential sales with conventional financing.

It's fair to assume that most of Carl's transactions have had those common characteristics. So, Carl's practice has been pretty much involved in wholesale violations of RESPA. Shame on Carl. He has been violating federal regulations. But have his actions been unethical?

---

[5] For reasons I cannot fathom, some people dispute this. In doing so, they contradict HUD, the agency charged with enforcing RESPA, and the opinions of, for one, the Legal Department of the California Association of Realtors®. The relevant section of RESPA is reproduced in Appendix 2.

It was noted in the first chapter that ethics and the law, while related, are certainly not what would be called coextensive. That is, not everything that is unethical is against the law, nor is everything that is against the law therefore unethical. (For example, it would be against the law for me to drive my car after the license plate tags had expired. But no one, I think, would call this unethical.)

Curiously, the Realtor® Code of Ethics does not specifically prohibit RESPA violations. The Code prohibits some kinds of behavior that are also illegal, such as discrimination in housing or failing to disclose material facts, but it does not have any general provisions that would say something like, "Realtors® shall obey all state and federal laws that apply to real estate transactions." It does not prohibit RESPA violations, nor does the Code prohibit the payment of referrals.[6]

Still, I believe that Carl's behavior, and that of anyone who acts similarly, is unethical as well as illegal. There may not be a formal "proof" available in support of my view, but there are factors to be considered.

While we all may agree that there are all sorts of laws that could be broken without being unethical, it seems to be different if the law-breaking has the characteristic of being persistent or repeated, and done simply for one's own self-interest. Such flouting of the law has the character, in and of itself, of being unethical.

Tom Morris, one of the most respected business ethics philosophers in the U.S., offers a handy little *six tests of ethical action*. "These," he says, "are simple tests we can use to evaluate the ethical appropriateness of actions." One of those six is what he calls "the publicity test." "Would I want to see this action described on the front page of the local paper?" or "How would I feel about having done this if everyone,

---

[6] It may seem surprising to some that the Code does not specifically prohibit illegal behavior. There is good reason for this. If it did, then it would be possible for an association of Realtors® to find a person guilty of violating the law. But this is a determination that associations are not civilly empowered to do. Such a finding could probably be challenged in court, with the association taking on considerable liability.

including the people I love, were to find out?"

If breaking a law—such as violating RESPA's anti-kickback provisions—is something you wouldn't want to see published in the local paper about yourself, then it meets Morris' test as being unethical.

Finally, there is what we might call the "level playing field" objection. It is not a level playing field when those who abide by the rules have to compete against those who don't (and there is no attentive referee). Carl has unfairly obtained a competitive advantage over other agents who operate within the restrictions of the law. We can't believe that Carl would want others to be able to illicitly obtain advantages over him. To be sure, none of us *wants* others to beat us out in competition. But most of us find that acceptable as long as everyone is playing by the rules. Assuming that Carl is like the rest of us in that regard, his actions don't pass the Golden Rule test.

3

Listings

"Old Realtors® never die, they just grow listless." The point, of course, is that listings are the lifeblood of the real estate business. It may all start with prospecting, but that prospecting needs to result in listings.

To be sure, some agents restrict their practice to working with buyers only. And some of them are quite, and deservedly, successful. Still, for the vast majority, listings are the key to survival and success.

The relationship between sellers and their listing agents is a complex one. Under most arrangements, the agent is a fiduciary of the seller. That legal obligation, along with the requirements of Article I of the Realtor® Code of Ethics, obligates the agent to promote the interests of sellers, to put their interests first. This is not always easy. Often, that is simply because, in the case of a conflict, it would not be instinctive to most people to give primary consideration to another.

But there are other, more subtle, reasons that it is not always easy to promote the client's interests. Frequently, the clients themselves may not know what is in their best interest. It is not unusual for the client's thoughts to be based on misinformation. Hence, it is often the case that a large part of the listing and pre-listing relationship consists in the education of the seller by the Realtor®.

Moreover, the listing relationship can also be strained because the agent has other obligations as well as that of promoting the client's interest. Article 1 also obligates the agent to treat all parties honestly. Agents also have both ethical and legal obligations with respect to disclosures. More than one seller has felt that the listing agent was acting almost as an adversary, because the agent was insistent on fulfilling disclosure obligations to the buyer. Sometimes, hard as it is to believe, this is not what some sellers want. Some sellers have actually been known to desire to deceive the buyer about something, and they may want their agent to be a party to this deception. An ethical agent cannot do that, even though he or she is a fiduciary of the seller.

There is no shortage of articles and media commentaries that employ broad-brush criticisms of the intentions and behavior of real estate listing agents. Some otherwise bright people are liable to say some really stupid things about the greed and self-serving behavior of listing agents in general.[7] While such criticisms are usually exaggerated and overly broad, we in the business need to acknowledge that they don't come from nowhere. There is usually some truth, albeit perhaps not as dramatic, behind them.

It is, for example, an ongoing irony of the real estate business that many seasoned agents employ, and many new agents are taught, a variety of dubious ploys and stratagems that are designed to induce a potential seller into listing with them. Whether it's "We have a buyer [or *buyers*] for your home" or "Highest Price Guaranteed," the tag lines usually don't mean exactly what they appear to mean. They are, quite bluntly, tricks; and using a trick seems more than a little problematic as a means of trying to create a fiduciary relationship.

We need to be as ethical in obtaining a listing as we should be in carrying out its duties.

Underpriced

Yes, indeed, the real estate gods were smiling on Marci today. Not an hour after she had come in for floor time, there, right out of the blue, came a "come-list-me" call. The lady on the phone, Ethel, explained that, although she didn't know any of the agents at Cold Creek Realty, she knew its reputation as the top real estate company in town. "As a matter of fact," Ethel explained, "I haven't lived in Four Oaks for some time. But Cold Creek Realty was *the* office when we lived here, and I

---

[7] For a critique of one of these commentaries, see Bob Hunt, "Why Do Agents' Homes Sell for More?" *Realty Times*, January 8, 2007.

see it still has signs all over the place. Can you come by to see my property this afternoon?" *Of course.*

It was natural for Marci to be a bit nervous as she strode up to the front porch. Still, she was confident too. She had her freshly minted CMA in hand—not bad for a "newbie" (four months in the business) to have cranked out in the last two hours of her floor time. Although the comps weren't ideal—nothing had sold in this immediate neighborhood for the past few months—the ones she had used would probably satisfy any appraiser. Besides, Mark, who had a few years of real estate under his belt, had given the CMA a quick once-over and pronounced it OK. Based on the comps, and the tax data about the house, depending upon its condition it should go for somewhere in the range of $160,000 to $185,000.

Ethel opened the door before Marci could even ring the bell, and took charge immediately. "Young lady," she said, "I see that you have brought along all your folders and papers and fancy brochures, and I appreciate that. But let me tell you, you don't need them. I know your company, and I know you must be a good real estate lady or they wouldn't have hired you. So you don't have to convince me of anything —you have the listing."

"Now," she went on, "let me tell you about the price I want. Although I haven't lived here for a while, I've kept in touch with my old neighbors. Irma Varsek, over on Lincoln, told me that Alex Forbes got $130,000 for his place just last year, and I have one more bedroom than he did. Imagine, $130,000 for Alex's place! Why, before my Henry died—rest his soul—he and I said that if we could ever get $90,000 for this place, we'd sell it and retire to Hawaii.

"But that's how things were then. Times have changed, and don't think I don't know it. I've already talked this over with the children, Ben in California and Earl in Michigan; and they agree. I want $140,000 for this place, and I won't take a penny less."

The rest of the listing appointment—if that's what you would call it—was pretty much a blur for Marci. Ethel took her on a tour of the house, told her about the tenants who had lived there the past five years, gave her a key, and asked her to please go quickly with the paperwork. She was going to meet an old friend for tea.

The paperwork was fine. Ethel crossed out the 180-day listing period and made it 90, but Marci didn't mind at all. She was out the door and on her way back to the office in less than an hour from the time she had arrived. Marci had her first listing, and, at a price of $140,000, she was confident that she would soon have her first sale.

Marci's confidence was well placed. "Oh, Ethel," she excitedly spoke into the phone just two days later, "I am so happy for you—and I know your Henry would be happy too. We have just received a full-price offer on your house!"

Underpriced: Comments and Analysis

We all love to have well-priced listings, and if they are on the lower end of well-priced, well, then, so much the better. But underpriced? That's something else.

First, and for the sake of discussion, let's concede that Marci's listing was underpriced. I know, I know: "Only the market can tell us what the right price is." "Valuation is not an exact science." Etc., etc. Still, and for the sake of argument, let's agree that the $140,000 list price was definitely under market. (If that's still a struggle for you, how about $120,000?)

Was it wrong, unethical, to take the listing at that price? Remember, after all, it was Ethel who set the price, not Marci. Nor did Marci say anything dishonest to Ethel or actively try to mislead her in any way.

Still, what Marci did—and that includes what she failed to do—was unethical. Article 1 of the Code of Ethics says this:

> When representing a buyer, seller, landlord, tenant, or
> other client as an agent, Realtors® pledge themselves to
> protect and promote the interests of their client. This
> obligation to the client is primary, but it does not
> relieve Realtors® of their obligation to treat all parties

> honestly. When serving a buyer, seller, landlord, tenant
> or other party in a non-agency capacity, Realtors®
> remain obligated to treat all parties honestly.

It obligates a Realtor® "to protect and promote the interests of their client." Sure, Marci did what Ethel asked her to do; but that's not necessarily the same as protecting and promoting Ethel's interests. Sometimes people can be mistaken about what is in their interest, because they are ignorant of the relevant facts. By every indication, that's what Ethel's situation was. It wasn't that she just didn't care about money (remember: "I won't take a penny less!") Rather, she had incompetently judged the marketplace.

What might Marci have done? She really should have tried to educate Ethel about what appeared to be an appropriate market price for her property. She should have used her CMA, and, if that didn't work, she might have suggested that Ethel hire an independent appraiser.

So what if Marci did all these things and Ethel persisted in wanting to list at $140,000? Neither the Code of Ethics nor ethics in general requires us to make everything right in the world. We need to do the best we can, but having done that, we go on. Indeed, if Marci had made a good-faith effort at informing Ethel and encouraging her to list for more, and Ethel still refused, we would then have to begin to wonder if price really were Ethel's number one priority. Maybe something else was going on. Anyway, if Marci did her best and was still unable to change Ethel's mind, then it would be perfectly acceptable to list it at the price Ethel named.

Those who are sensitive to risk management issues are liable to have some concern here. If it were the case that, even after Marci's explanations, Ethel was determined to stay at the low price, then it would be a very good idea for Marci to obtain some written and signed documentation of that fact. It need not be elaborate, but you'd want it to be clear that Ethel was advised of the agent's opinion that the market value of the home was significantly higher than the price at which Ethel wished to list it. Ethel might not care about getting full value, but you can bet that her heirs might care.

Interested readers might want to look at Cases 1-15 and 1-16 of the Case Interpretations of the Code of Ethics for elaboration of these points. But you can also come to similar conclusions by applying the general principle of the Golden Rule. Marci should treat Ethel as she (Marci) would want to be treated. And you'd have to be more than a little insincere to say "I want people to do what I want, so, by following the Golden Rule, I (Marci) should do what Ethel wants." None of us wants to be left to our own choices when those choices are based on misinformation that could result in harm to us. We'd rather be informed. And, by the principle of the Golden Rule, Marci should have informed Ethel.

Exclusive Office Listing

How sweet it is: to take a well-priced listing of a good property during a red-hot seller's market. And Ken was savoring the sweetness.

"Well, Mr. and Mrs. Reynolds ..."

"Please, Ken, it's Don and Linda."

"OK, then, Don and Linda, we just about have everything wrapped up. We've set a price, and we've listed your fine property for a period of ninety days—not that we're going to need ninety days—and we've gone over the disclosure documents you'll need to complete. There's just a little bit more paperwork to complete, and I think you are really going to like this."

"We're going to like the paperwork? I can't imagine that."

"Well, no, Don, I guess I didn't state that quite right. It's not that you'll like the paperwork—there's only a one-page form to sign anyway—but you are going to like what it represents."

"You see, because your house is so nice ..."

"We always have tried to keep things up."

"Yes, well, because you have maintained this lovely home so well, it will qualify for our company's Exclusive Office Listing Program.

"You see, most homes are not nearly as nice as yours, and that's why most homes don't qualify for our program. If a home is just average, or below average, well, then, we have to expose it to the whole market-place. We have to let every possible buyer and agent know about it, in the hopes of finding someone who will come along and be interested.

"And let me tell you, when a property gets full exposure like that, it's no picnic for the owners. For one thing, you get agents calling or coming to the house who haven't even seen it yet. And, I'm sorry to say, there are a lot of agents out there who just aren't as professional as the ones in our company. They'll call you just about any time of the day or night, and they'll expect you to let them show it at the drop of a hat.

"And that's not all. When a home gets the full exposure treatment, you're liable to have people show up who don't even have an agent. They'll see your home and its address on the Internet, or they'll drive by and see a sign, and they'll just come up to your door. If you can imagine. Total strangers!

"Fortunately, your home is so nice that we don't have to tell every Tom, Dick, and Harry about it. We don't need to scrape the bottom of the barrel for buyers. Which is great, because you certainly don't want all that hassle and bother. And we don't want you to have to go through it.

"Our job is to represent you and to look out for your interests, just like I told you when I explained the agency form. We want to protect you, and we want to make this whole process easy for you. That's what the Exclusive Office Listing Program is all about."

"Oh, Ken, we are so happy we listed with you and your company."

"Well, thank you, Linda; but let me explain this a little bit more. When your home is exclusively listed with us, then we keep the information about it in our company so that it is available only to our highly professional agents. Otherwise, we'd have to put it in the multiple listing, and, again I'm sorry to say it, unfortunately the standards for being a multiple listing agent are not set very high.

"With the Exclusive Office Listing Program, you won't have a bunch of strangers going through your home. Buyers will be only with our agents, so you'll know you are being looked out for.

"Now, of course we'll still advertise. That's one of the reasons there's a minimum thirty-day period to be in the program, so that we can get into publication cycles and be sure it appears in our exclusive company booklet—I'm sure you've seen them around town—and we can post your property on our company Internet site. I'm even going to run my own personal ads for you in both of the newspapers.

"So, you see, lots of potential buyers will be able to learn about your property. But the beauty of this program is that they have to come through our agents, so we can be sure everything will be handled professionally and in your interest."

"Well, I guess we are really glad now that we have kept the house up so well. Right, Linda? Ken, where do we sign?"

"Right at the bottom of this form, Don. The form just says that I have explained our program to you, and I have explained how everybody in the world finds out about your house when it is on multiple listing, and that you prefer to be with our program."

"It makes sense to me, Ken. Heck, isn't this what they call a 'no-brainer'?"

Exclusive Office Listing: Comments and Analysis

We all know why Ken—more precisely, Ken's company—wanted the Reynoldses to sign up for the Exclusive Office Listing Program.[8] It is because an exclusive office listing of this sort gives the company a better shot at double-ending the transaction—receiving both the listing

---

[8] Here, *exclusive office listing* is being used to mean that the property is not offered on the MLS or other cooperative system and that only the individual agent and/or agents from the listing office will be showing it to prospective buyers. It is sometimes called a "pocket listing" or "office exclusive."

and selling sides of the commission. If other brokers and agents in the MLS don't have information about or access to the property, that almost guarantees that an agent from Ken's company—maybe even Ken himself—will be the one to bring an offer.

Is it a bad thing for the transaction to be double-ended? No, unless you have a particular problem with dual agency or your state law prohibits it. But it certainly is, or could be, a bad thing to reduce the exposure of the property. Doing so just decreases the likelihood of prospective buyers learning about the house. Doing so also decreases the likelihood of the owners receiving the best possible offer.

Some will argue that there may be a problem with exclusive office listings in a slow or even normal market, but there is no harm done by them in a hot seller's market. "The property generally gets sold right away, so what's the problem?" Well, the problem is not that it takes longer for the property to sell; rather, it is that, without adequate exposure, the seller may not receive as high a price.

A characteristic of a strong seller's market is that properties are liable to receive multiple offers. Frequently, this may result in the property ultimately being sold for even more than the listed price. A bidding war may take place. But the likelihood of that, and the number of potential bidders, is greatly reduced if the property is not exposed through some kind of cooperative marketing service like an MLS.

It is common for a multiple listing service to require that members enter a listing into the database within a specified time frame, e.g., within 48 hours of taking the listing. If a property is not to be entered within the required period, the MLS may require that the listing brokerage submit or have on file a waiver from the seller. Typically, the waiver would contain an acknowledgment by the seller that the benefits of exposure through the MLS had been explained to them.

But such waivers easily become just one more item in that pile of documents that principals sign without really reading or thinking about them. The form that Ken had Mr. and Mrs. Reynolds sign could easily have contained the requisite language. And, had there been an ethics hearing, Ken might have testified that he *did* explain to them how putting their property in the MLS would have given it more exposure. But it's hard to imagine that his testimony would be very persuasive.

Article 3 of the Code of Ethics provides that Realtors® shall cooperate with other brokers, *except when cooperation is not in the client's best interest.* And it is certainly possible that there can be situations where cooperation might not be in the client's best interest. (See, for example, Code of Ethics Case Interpretation 3-4.) But it's pretty unlikely. Certainly, people can be *persuaded* that they don't want to have the exposure that comes about through broker cooperation. That is what happened in this scenario, and it is wrong. Moreover, there are plenty of people—not really understanding how the marketplace works—who may start out thinking that broker cooperation is not worth the trouble (and, indeed, it may cause more inconvenience), or who say, "I just want your company to sell it." In such cases, a conscientious Realtor® will make a sincere effort to explain to them the benefits of broker cooperation. If the client still declines, so be it; but the Realtor® needs to have made a good-faith effort to present the facts.

Presumptively, broker cooperation is in the client's best interest. Ken certainly did not attempt to explain that to the Reynoldses. Indeed, his pitch was a deliberate attempt to mislead them. In that, his behavior was contrary both to Article 3 and to Article 1. He certainly wasn't putting their interests first.

Even without the articles, his actions definitely flouted the Golden Rule.

Overpriced

Of course, Eric had butterflies. This was his first listing interview, after all those weeks of door knocking and sending mailers. Maybe it was finally going to start paying off.

He was as prepared as anyone could be. He knew the comps cold, and he knew the model and floor plan of the home he was going to. His

CMA was a piece of art, and it demonstrated clearly and convincingly that the Lloyds' home would be in a range of $300,000 to $325,000.

In a way, though, that part didn't matter. Eric's broker had taught him otherwise. "Don't give them a price," Luis had told him, as he told all the new agents; "find out what they want." "Keep your eye on the prize," was Luis' counsel. And the prize was to get the listing, regardless of the price.

"Look," Luis had said, "everyone who interviews three or four agents—like the newspaper columnists tell them to do—has two objectives. They want to know who will get them the highest price, and, to them, that means who will list it the highest. And they want to pay the lowest commission. Don't you worry about the commission part; I'll show you how to take care of that. You just remember your scripts, find out what they're thinking, and *Get That Listing!*"

It was a good thing Eric hadn't come in with a recommended listing price. He and Roland Stevens would have been *very* far apart.

Eric had barely begun to go into his presentation when Roland began to rant about the first two agents he had interviewed. They both had no sense of value whatsoever. One of them didn't show any appreciation for the koi ponds and connecting streams that formed the centerpiece of the Stevenses' rear yard. Why, those had set Roland back more than $25,000! And yet that agent didn't even take them into account when suggesting a listing price.

The other agent was even worse. All he could do was fixate on the Greens' house down the street that had sold three weeks ago. It was the same model on a similar-size lot. It had sold for $318,000. "Do you know what, Eric?" Roland practically shouted. "All that the Greens did to get ready to sell was to put in new carpet and paint. Their landscaping was plain, but decent, but they hadn't done anything to the interior since they bought the house from the builder five years ago."

"And then look at everything we have done, all of which that other agent hardly seemed to notice. We put that custom wood paneling in the family room—it reminds me of the cabin—and there's the Murphy bed we had installed in the loft where Grandma stays sometimes. And the bedrooms—just look at them—each with its own distinctive color and carpeting. You think that didn't cost a pretty penny? Yet all that other agent could do was to talk about the Greens' house."

Eric completed a tour of the Stevenses' home, listening to Roland tout the worth of their various "improvements." Along the way, he was able to discern that the price in Roland's mind was a lot closer to $400,000 than it was to $300,000.

When they were through, and Eric had done his presentation, Roland was insistent. "Well, Eric, what do you think we ought to list it for?" Without skipping a beat, Eric confidently replied that $385,000 seemed like the right figure to him.

"You know," Roland responded, "before you came in here, I was pretty sure that $375,000 would be about right; but I can see that you are a perceptive young man who understands value. It's going to be a pleasure doing business with you."

The rest of the appointment went quickly and easily. Getting the 6% commission was a cinch, given Eric's mastery of the script and Roland's happiness with the price. The company's six-month listing policy was no problem either. Indeed, it was practically a textbook conversation.

Eric knew there would be plenty of time for the subsequent conversations about market conditions, today's buyers who had no appreciation for quality, and the negative influence of other agents who, likewise, had no appreciation or understanding. He'd eventually get the price down to a place where it would sell; everyone would be happy (well, pretty much); and he would be sending out his first "Just Sold" cards in the neighborhood. In the meantime, he would reap all the visibility in the neighborhood from his listing cards, the sign, and open-house activity. He was on his way.

Overpriced: Comments and Analysis

In many respects, the issues about overpricing are similar to those about underpricing. Most notably, we need to acknowledge again that valuing and pricing a property is not an exact science. We can't always be sure.[9] Although there clearly *are* some circumstances that warrant a greater degree of certainty than others. For the sake of argument, though, let us stipulate here that a $385,000 price was too high by a good deal, and Eric knew it.

Before delving into the ethical issues here, it might be worthwhile to address a question that might occur to some readers: Why would anyone deliberately want to take an overpriced listing anyway?

Agents will differ on this point. Some will agree with the implicit premise of the question. They will tell you that overpriced listings are the scourge of the business. They waste time and money, and are bad for your mental health. I tend to be in this camp myself.

Others, though, will look at it the way Eric and his broker do: An overpriced listing is better than no listing at all. Its value is threefold. For one thing, if the agent plays his cards right, he stands a good chance of getting the price reduced—sometimes more than once—until it becomes saleable. Secondly, a listing gives an agent visibility. There's nothing like having "For Sale" signs in your farm or around town. Third, even an overpriced listing can be an excellent lead generator due to buyer calls and open-house activity.

So, given that Roland had an inflated idea of his home's value anyway, did Eric really do anything wrong? We have to say, "Yes." Unlike Marci, in the earlier case of underpricing, Eric affirmatively and knowingly quoted a price that was considerably beyond the market. To be sure, the seller was inclined in that direction anyway, but that is still no excuse for Eric's active falsehood.

---

[9] My favorite example of this occurred some years ago when the market had hit a brick wall and interest rates were soaring. I saw two professional appraisals of a very plush condominium that were more than $100,000 apart. *And they had both used the same comparables!*

But, suppose the situation had been slightly different. Suppose that Roland hadn't asked for Eric's price opinion. He might have just announced that he was certain of its value, say $375,000—which was still too high—and wanted to know if Eric would list it at that price. Would it have been wrong for Eric simply to say, "Yes," and to get on with it?

In such a circumstance, Eric would still be shirking his ethical duty.

Standard of Practice 1-3 says:

> Realtors®, in attempting to secure a listing, shall not deliberately mislead the owner as to market value.

Now, if Eric were going along with Roland's price, he might not be guilty of deliberately misleading Roland (see also Code of Ethics Case Interpretation 1-17), but he still wouldn't be fulfilling his Article 1 duty to protect and promote the interests of his client. As we have noted earlier, putting the client's interest first does not simply equate to doing what the client asks or says he wants.

Much of what Realtors® do, especially in listing situations, is to educate their clients. It's just a fact: Principals (sellers *and* buyers) frequently don't know as much about the market as they think they do. Sellers especially often are acquainted with only a slice of the relevant data. They are frequently influenced by the opinions of all sorts of people who, themselves, are not knowledgeable; and, for sure, they read the newspapers selectively when the topic is real estate.

Doing the educating is not always fun. It often requires tact and some very careful phrasing, but it is something we owe to those who would entrust us with so much influence over the disposal of their assets. Without good information, no one can make informed decisions. So, it's back to the Golden Rule as well as Article 1. What would *we* want if the roles were reversed? It wouldn't be simply to have an agent go along with whatever wrong-headed idea we might have. It would be to be given the information on which we could base a good decision.

Suppose, though, that Eric made every tactful effort to educate Roland about his home's value, and that it was all to no avail. This happens.

Often. Would it then be wrong for Eric to take the listing at an inflated price? No. Just as we noted with respect to the person who was undervaluing her house, we have an obligation to try to keep people from being misled, but if they persist in their ideas, that can't be our ethical burden.

If you say, "Mr. Jones, I think this price is more than is indicated by the present market (or something to that effect), but I will take the listing and I will work on it as diligently as I can," then that's just fine.

But, as we noted with the underpricing case, it would be a good idea from a risk management perspective to obtain a written record of this. Also, and this isn't solely an ethical point, it would be a good idea to write down a plan, with dates, for reviewing the market activity—or lack thereof—and giving future consideration to a price reduction. That would be helpful to both you and your client.

4

Advertising

Just as *prospecting* is not a precise term, we must acknowledge that *advertising* isn't either. Nor, for that matter, is *marketing*. But that is not a problem for our purposes here. We are not doing a semantic study; we just want to consider some of the ethical issues that arise in the context of those activities that most of us would call *advertising*.

Probably the most familiar form of real estate advertising is that where some sort of representation through media (Internet, newspapers, television, mailings, etc.) is made for the purpose of interesting people in a particular property. For example:

> *Well-priced 3 bdr., 2 bath home in a great location. Nice yard, xlnt condition. Call today! 888-555-1212*

Ads like this have caused one wag to comment, "The same house is for sale all over the United States!"

Of course, properties aren't the only thing that we advertise. We advertise our companies, and we advertise ourselves. In all of the different kinds of advertising we do, there are both professional and legal guidelines to be followed. The lines may not always be exactly clear, but we need to be aware when we are close to them.

Within the realm of advertising, there is a phenomenon known as *puffery*. *Webster's* calls puffery "exaggerated commendation especially for promotional purposes," but that definition is a little sparse. More to the point is *Wikipedia's* "promotional statements and claims that express subjective rather than objective views, *such that no reasonable person would take them literally*" [my emphasis]. Finally, there is this from the Federal Trade Commission (FTC):

> [Puffery is a] term frequently used to denote the exaggerations reasonably to be expected of a seller as to the degree of quality of his product, the truth or falsity of which cannot be precisely determined.

Moreover, the FTC declared in its 1984 Policy Statement on Deception:

> The Commission generally will not pursue cases involving obviously exaggerated or puffing representations, i.e. those that the ordinary consumers do not take seriously.

What's crucial about puffery is that, for it to qualify as such, the consumer must "get it." It must be a representation so obviously exaggerated or vague that no one will be inclined to believe it or be misled by it. Pretty obviously, it is not always going to be clear whether or not a given ad or tagline is puffery.

In 2004, the United States Court of Appeal for the Eighth Circuit ruled in favor of a puffery defense in the case of *American Italian Pasta Co. v. New World Pasta Co.* New World had complained that it was false and misleading advertising for American to use the phrase "America's Favorite Pasta" in connection with the marketing of one of its product lines. The court ruled that the phrase fell into the category of "exaggerated statements of bluster or boast upon which no reasonable consumer would rely"—that is, that it was puffery and therefore not prohibited.

Some, of course, might dispute the court's finding in that regard. They might not think that the phrase "America's favorite pasta" was an obvious exaggeration. They might even think that some sort of survey or preference test stood behind it.

Be that as it may, the Realtor® Code of Ethics holds Realtor® advertising to a higher standard than does the law. Article 12 of the Realtor® Code of Ethics says:

> Realtors® shall be careful at all times to present a true picture in their advertising and representations to the public. Realtors® shall also ensure that their professional status (e.g., broker, appraiser, property manager, etc.) or status as Realtor® is clearly identifiable in any such advertising.

No exceptions are granted for puffery. If an ad is such an obvious exaggeration that ordinary consumers would not take it seriously, it might be legal because it is puffery, but it would not be ethical because it does not present a "true picture." (In particular, see Case Interpretation 12-2.)

Advertising involves other things beyond making claims. Sometimes, it also involves what has been called *targeting*. Most obviously, ads are targeted to certain audiences by the selection of the medium in which the ad appears. An ad for horse property in *Equestrian Magazine* would be targeted to a particular audience. Targeting makes good sense, and there is nothing inherently wrong with it.

Targeting may occur in other ways as well. The uses of models and settings in a visual ad may be intended to tell viewers who the product is for or who would be a likely purchaser of the product. There's a reason you don't see many twenty-somethings in ads for cruise ship lines. Again, targeting in advertising is not something that in and of itself is illegal or unethical. But it can be if the targeting is indicative of some kind of discriminatory preference. This also is an area where the guidelines to be followed are somewhat less than crystal clear, but we need to be aware of them and to avoid crossing them as best we can.

Exaggerations

Elena wasn't surprised that Ed wanted to interview different agents before they chose one to list their house. She didn't think it mattered herself. She had told him so too.

"What difference does it make? They all do the same thing: They put the information in that multi-list, or whatever they call it; they put a sign in our front yard, run some ads in the newspaper, and hope someone comes along and buys it. But there really isn't a dime's worth of difference between them. Why don't we just give the listing to that nice young man who sends us postcards and puts little flags in our front yard every Fourth of July?"

But, oh, no, not Mr. Engineer. "You'd better not be right about that, Elena, because if you are, they are sure wasting a lot of money with all those ads and mailers that say why this guy's the best, or this company's the best, or how you can make so much more money with so and so. No, I want to check these people out, and then we'll make our decision on which one we think is the best."

On reflection, the first interview—the one with Jennifer—hadn't really been that bad. It just seemed awfully uncomfortable to Elena at the time. But, then, that happened with lots of Ed's conversations. Maybe "interrogations" would be a better word.

"Jennifer, I want to ask you about that postcard you sent us recently, the one with the graphs," Ed began, innocently enough. "There, splashed across the top of the graph, it says 'We're Number One!' but, then, down below the graph, and in pretty small print too, it says that this is a comparison of local, independent real estate companies. What do you mean by that, Jennifer?"

"That's a good question, Mr. Sanders, and I'm glad you asked me," Jennifer responded without hesitation. "What that means is that we are comparing apples to apples here. Each company represented on the graph is locally owned. There are none of those big companies that are part of some national chain, and there aren't any of those franchise companies there either."

"That's all well and good," said Ed, his voice getting just a little edgy now, "but if you think it's important for me to know that you are number one among *that* group, don't you think I'd like to know who is really number one, when compared to everybody? Who is number one, Jennifer? As a matter of fact, where does your company rank when we consider the whole pack?"

Elena rescued that conversation by offering Jennifer some tea and then steering the talk to Jennifer's career—how long she'd been in real estate, how it worked out with her family, etc. After a while, they parted amicably, and Jennifer even came away thinking she might have a chance at the listing.

Come to think of it, the interview with Jennifer might have been the easiest of them all. Certainly the worst was with those people who had advertised that they would put more money—a lot more money—into a seller's pocket. They had said they would do that by charging only a 1% commission.

"You mean if I get $400,000 for this place, I'm going to have to pay you real estate people only $4,000?" Ed queried. Then when they got into the particulars about how he would also have to pay a cooperating broker, and it would probably be more than 1%, Ed got a little testy, to say the least.

"First, you say I'm going to pay only a 1% commission; then you tell me I'm going to have to pay *two* commissions. Do you have any more little surprises for me?" Elena's offer of tea wasn't enough to rescue that conversation.

Then there was that poor man who arrived with such bearing and an air of self-confidence. "It says here," Ed began, holding up an ad from the real estate section, "that you are in the top 1% of all real estate agents in the country. That's very impressive. I didn't even know they ranked all the real estate agents in the country."

"Where do you think I would have come out if they ranked all the engineers, honey?" he directed to Elena, not really expecting—or getting—an answer.

"Well, Mr. Sanders, there really isn't an organization that ranks everyone in the real estate business ..."

"So, how the hell do you know you're in the top 1%?" Ed almost bellowed. He got that way occasionally.

The air of self-confidence was pretty much gone by then, but you did have to give the fellow some credit for trying to rescue his claim by saying how he could extrapolate by comparing himself to other agents who were in the top 1% of their national companies, and he knew that he did more business than they did, etc. Needless to say, though, it just didn't fly with Ed.

Finally, there was that poor couple who had sent them a mailer saying, "We have buyers for your house!" Their mailer told how they had sold a home one block over, and their ads had brought such a flock of buyers, that they apparently had someone who would buy Ed and Elena's house, and most of the neighbors' too.

It wasn't so much the fact that they wanted Ed and Elena to sign a listing agreement that got him going. He said he understood that they needed to have something in writing before they brought the buyer, or buyers, to the house. It was when they wanted it to be a six-month listing agreement. You don't want to hear the riot act he read them.

"I guess you were right, after all," he finally said one evening. "We might as well just list it with that guy who gives us the flags. But you know what? First, I'm going to call the realty board and tell them what I think about the advertising their people do."

Exaggerations: Comments and Analysis

Really, how many companies can be "Number One"? Presumably, all of them, if they are allowed to qualify that claim as Jennifer did. It's even a common topic for joking among real estate agents, as in "Oh, sure, we're the Number One company on the south side of the 400 block of East Main Street."

For some reason a lot of real estate companies and agents feel compelled to quantify their claims of success, and far too frequently those claims can't be substantiated, or, as in Jennifer's case, they need such qualification that they lose their significance.

It is not only ads using specific numbers or percentages that present a problem. Likewise, various claims and assertions such as "We have buyers for homes in your neighborhood" or "Save time and money by purchasing your home through Slick Realty" may not be true exactly as stated and may stand up only when qualified to a point of being practically meaningless.

Perhaps those who employ advertising like this would counter that these ads are just puffing—harmless exaggeration—and that there is nothing wrong with them. If this is meant to invoke the puffery defense that exists in the law, we need to remember that a key element of that notion is that the consumer must "get it." Something about it must make the exaggeration obvious or the claim so vague that no one would expect it to be taken literally.

Regardless of that, though, we remember that the puffery defense is a *legal* defense. And in this arena, professional ethics holds us to a higher standard than the law. All such advertising is a violation of Article 12's injunction, "Realtors® shall be careful at all times to present a true picture in their advertising and representations to the public."

Curiously, though, the damage that this kind of advertising does is not the damage that Article 12 is primarily meant to prevent. The obligation to present a "true picture" is meant to keep people (members of the public) from being misled. Moreover, the damage to be prevented is not simply the fact of being misled. The serious damages are the *consequences* of being misled, whereby people are liable to waste time, effort, and money.

The untrue pictures painted by most company and agent puff pieces and exaggerated claims are far less likely to cause that kind of damage. Why? Because, unfortunately, there has been so much of that kind of advertising that, for the most part, no one believes it or pays much attention to it. It is understood, to put it as politely as possible, as being "just so much bull."[10]

This is different from false advertising. False advertising misleads, because it is something that people, not knowing it is false, expect to be true. But, frankly, many people don't even have an expectation of truth when agents and companies make exaggerated and extravagant claims about themselves. They just expect it to be bull.

In that case, then, the public isn't damaged. But we are.

---

[10] An elegant analysis of this phenomenon and the mind-set that creates it is provided by Princeton Emeritus Professor of Philosophy Harry G. Frankfurt, *On Bullshit*, Princeton University Press, 2005.

Targeted Ad

Jeb Boyd was as close as anyone could be to a 21st century version of a "good old boy." Born and raised in Magnolia Hills, he was the first-born son of Jeremiah (Jerry) Randolph Boyd, likewise a native of Magnolia Hills, and a graduate of Macedonia College (now, Macedonia University).

Of course, Jerry Boyd had attended Macedonia in the "good old days," when it was an all-white, all-male school. Founded in the late 1800s, Macedonia's mission was "to educate white, Christian men and to prepare them for their positions of leadership in society."

When Jeb was there in the 1990s, everything had changed. That's why it didn't really bother Jerry when Jeb dropped out, citing the difference between what he had expected—based on his father's stories—and the way things were now. In Jerry's view, it seemed like Macedonia no longer stood for the natural order of things; there just wasn't any respect for tradition anymore. Having to compete with females in the classroom only compounded the problem.

Still, even with its changes, Macedonia University was at the center of Magnolia Hills' cultural and economic life. If ever there was a college town, Magnolia Hills was it. And that was a fact not lost on local entrepreneurs and businessmen.

It was exhilarating, though not a great surprise, that Jeb was able to obtain the property management and lease/rental listings on Harry Anderson's brand-new 8-unit building just two blocks from the campus. Harry reminded Jeb that it was Jeb's dad, Jerry, who had got Harry started in the real estate development business. "I owe a lot to him, Jeb, and now that you have taken over the business, I'm happy to be able to pay a little back by bringing business to you. We Macedonia guys always stick together."

It was a beautiful building, and, in Jeb's opinion, it would rent up easily. As he and Harry went over the rental rates, only one problem cropped up, but, fortunately, it was a little one. "Jeb," Harry said quite matter-of-factly, "I want to rent to college students—oh, excuse me,

University students—I've always done that, and I've always thought it was one way I could give something back to the school. But, I'll tell you, I don't want to rent to some of the kinds of students they have there now. I don't know what this world's coming to; but I don't have to support it. So you just find me some nice Caucasian Christian college boys. Don't you bother bringing me applications from no women, or coloreds, or Muslims, or gays, or radicals, or any of those kind; 'cause I just won't rent to them."

Jeb had heard this kind of thinking before. He couldn't have lived all his life in Magnolia Hills without hearing it. But he also knew that times were different, the laws were different, and you just couldn't do things the way you did in the old days. "Mr. Anderson, I'll tell you I know how you feel, and I'm here do what you want, but I have to let you know that we can't say what you just said without getting in a whole heap of trouble. The laws are different now, in real estate just like everything else. So I'm going to have to be pretty careful in the ads that I write and the way I screen tenants. But don't you worry. I'm going to get you what you want, but we just can't be so blatant about it."

Jeb was so proud of the ad he crafted. He should have stuck around the school and been a writing major!

> *Looking for traditional Macedonia students who value the school's heritage to occupy plush units in an exclusive new building conveniently close to campus and the First Baptist Church. Nonstudent applicants must supply satisfactory employment verification. Proximity to campus gym and jogging trails makes this location perfect for active young men.*

The ad didn't specify that any particular type of tenant would be unwelcome, and yet readers should get the message. Macedonia students were, after all, pretty smart; they should be able to read between the lines. Of course, Jeb would still have to weed out some applicants, but, on the whole, he should get the type of tenant Harry Anderson was looking for.

Jeb was dismayed when he received a notification from the MLS that his listing input had been rejected because of the wording in the Remarks section. He stormed over to the board office and demanded an explanation.

"Jeb, you just can't say things like this anymore," stammered Jody, the all-purpose staff member.

"What do you mean?" demanded Jeb, "This is exactly the same wording that I sent to the paper, and they didn't have a problem with it! The MLS turns it down? That's ridiculous. The MLS isn't even an advertising publication. I'm going to demand a hearing with the board of directors!"

"Well, Jeb," sweet Jody responded, "I think you're going to have a hearing, but not the one you're looking for. We've already had a complaint from someone who saw the ad in the paper."

Targeted Ad: Comments and Analysis

Discrimination is wrong. We know this because we know that we wouldn't want to be discriminated against. It's a simple Golden Rule application. Discrimination is also against the law. The major fair housing laws are included in the Civil Rights Act of 1968. There are also other federal and state laws governing this subject. Moreover, there are extensive stipulations regarding discrimination in the Realtor® Code of Ethics.

Article 10 of the Realtor® Code of Ethics says this:

> Realtors® shall not deny equal professional services
> to any person for reasons of race, color, religion, sex,
> handicap, familial status, or national origin. Real-
> tors® shall not be parties to any plan or agreement to
> discriminate against a person or persons on the basis
> of race, color, religion, sex, handicap, familial status,
> or national origin.

Even more pertinent to our scenario is Standard of Practice 10-3:

> Realtors® shall not print, display or circulate any state-
> ment or advertisement with respect to selling or renting
> of a property that indicates any preference, limitations or
> discrimination based on race, color, religion, sex, handi-
> cap, familial status, or national origin.

Discrimination is not always blatant. Often it is subtle or indirect, but
no less wrong—either legally or morally. Indeed, some have said that
subtle, unacknowledged discrimination can be even more hurtful than
discrimination out in the open.

Although there is nothing in the Realtor® Code of Ethics or the Case
Interpretations that gets down to specific language that might be
considered discriminatory, there is a considerable body of opinion and
guidelines on the subject that has been developed by various federal
and state agencies. Additionally, newspapers and other media outlets
have developed their own guidelines. Unfortunately, though, these
privately developed guidelines don't always match those created by the
government agencies.

Plenty of myths and urban legends have developed concerning these
topics. For example, many people are under the impression that an ad
shouldn't include a phrase like "family room" because that would
indicate a preference for, or bias against, certain kinds of lifestyles.
That particular alleged ban has been disavowed by the Department of
Housing and Urban Development. Nonetheless, one can understand
how people could think such things. For an example of one of these
word lists, see Appendix 3.

Consider the ad that Jeb wrote:

> *Looking for traditional Macedonia students who value the
> school's heritage to occupy plush units in an exclusive new
> building conveniently close to campus and the First Baptist
> Church. Nonstudent applicants must supply satisfactory
> employment verification. Proximity to campus gym and
> jogging trails makes this location perfect for active young
> men.*

From a fair housing agency point of view, the analysis might run something like this:

> The appeal to "traditional Macedonia students" can certainly be construed to signal a preference for the type of student it has had through most of its history—white, male, and Christian. Calling the building "exclusive" signals that certain types of applicants will not be accepted. Indicating its proximity to the First Baptist Church indicates a preference for certain religious types. The last sentence clearly suggests that the owner is trying to appeal to the nonhandicapped, and it clearly states a gender preference.

And of course it can go on and on. Note that nothing was mentioned in the analysis about nonstudents submitting employment verification. What do you think? Does that raise a red flag also?

Jeb was upset that the MLS had a problem with his ad (probably entered as the Remarks section in the listing), whereas the newspaper had accepted it. Two comments: First, that's the newspaper's problem. They should have rejected it. Second, MLS systems are subject to the same guidelines as are newspapers. We can debate all we want as to whether or not putting a listing into the MLS is *advertising*; but it is well established that fair housing agencies will hold MLS systems accountable to the same standards. Moreover, treating an MLS entry as advertising has considerably more plausibility, now that MLS remarks appear on publicly viewed Internet sites.

New-Tract Buzz

Chad Hollings had been building homes in Pleasanton for more than fifteen years, but this was his first big project. Not that it was his first big home; he had just never taken on building so many. And, sure, to the big boys, an 18-home development was no big deal. That didn't constitute even one phase. But for Chad, it was big potatoes, and if he brought it off, there would be more.

The project was on a forty-two acre parcel that used to be a part of the Manley farm. As a matter of fact, Ed Manley had put up the land in a joint venture with Chad. The first four homes were done, another six were about two thirds finished, and he was getting ready to pour concrete for the remaining eight.

Things had not gone as planned or hoped for. It had been a long, hard winter; the models were only recently finished, and here it was June already. They just plain missed the early spring buying season. Still, though, Chad thought some of the homes would have been under contract by now. But, no—not one.

Nor could he figure out the problem. The product was good—he knew that. And with the growth that Pleasanton had been experiencing, he knew there was demand. Sure, the project was a little bit farther out of town than any existing neighborhoods, but neither he nor the bank thought that would be a significant barrier to sales—especially because no one seemed to have any problem driving to the new Super Wal-Mart, which was about the same distance from town on the other side.

He couldn't figure it out. He'd actually had plenty of traffic. Lookers had seen the billboard and the ads in the paper. They all seemed to like what they saw, but so far, not a single offer.

Chad had always thought that he would use a real estate agent for the last few sales, but he never expected to need to incur that expense at the beginning. He didn't have anything against them—he'd worked with agents plenty of times—but he couldn't see why he should pay their fees if he didn't need them. That tune had changed by now. He knew he needed help, and that's why he was meeting with Nell. Nell was an old friend and well-known as one of the most high-producing, aggressive salespeople in the area.

"Chad, you know me," Nell started right in. "I always like to cut to the chase. Look, I know you need me to help you market these homes. Things didn't work out quite the way you thought they would, and you're getting a little worried now. That's OK. I knew it would just be a matter of time.

"The truth is, Chad, you have a good product here, and we are going to get them all sold. But these puppies need to be marketed. They're not just going to sell themselves.

"And here's the deal. No one wants to be the first person to buy out here. You're a little ways out of town, and, sure, five years from now your homes will be surrounded; but, right now, people aren't sure about the location.

"So, you have to do something to help them have confidence. If no one wants to be the first buyer, you have to make it possible for them to be number three or number four."

"Nell, I'd love to have a couple of buyers already, but that's just my problem ..."

"Chad, honey, that's where I come in. I'll supply you with those first buyers. We'll get the pump primed, get some activity buzzing out here, and you'll be sold out before you finish those last eight houses!"

Nell knew what needed to be done, and she knew how to do it. Within a couple of weeks she had set up straw buyers for the first "sale." Chad carried a bogus note—which they would never pay—and the deed documentation was made to look as if they had paid full price. Nell even arranged for the newspaper to carry a little story and a photo of Chad and Nell handing them the keys.

During the same period, Nell posted "Sold" signs on four of the other homes under construction, including one on a lot where they hadn't even started framing yet. And, of course, "Sold" stickers marked those lots on the tract map at the sales office.

It worked like a charm. Activity probably tripled. Sales were made, and some folks even signed up to be in "backup" position on the ones that Nell had posted as sold. (And what do you know? All the backup buyers wound up being able to purchase the home they wanted.) Hardly anyone even noticed when those first buyers moved out (as planned) and the property went back to the builder, who rapidly resold it—at a higher price. The project sold out, just as Nell predicted. And everyone was happy.

New-Tract Buzz: Comments and Analysis

"Everyone was happy." Certainly, this would be one of Nell's defenses, should anyone challenge her ethics for the way she operated. (She might also argue that plenty of others do the same thing.) No one got hurt; so where's the wrong?

We have noted before that *results* aren't the only determiners of right and wrong. Things can turn out badly even though no one did anything wrong. Conversely, someone can act wrongly, yet no one is harmed. It happens, albeit not very often.

Are "Sold" signs advertising? To be sure, they do convey what one might consider *neutral* information, but certainly they are used for advertising purposes as well. (See Case Interpretation 12-5.) In any case, Nell had also arranged for a newspaper story which certainly had an advertising element to it. That and the "Sold" signs were part of a coordinated advertising campaign. If Article 12's "true picture" injunction has any meaning to it at all, it was clearly violated by Nell.

Moreover, in this case, as in so many others, even without appealing to the Realtor® Code of Ethics, we know by applying the Golden Rule that Nell was ethically out of line. Put yourself in the shoes of, say, the second or third buyer. Would you have wanted to know the truth? Would you be content with being deceived?

Finally, it's important to take note of Nell's action with respect to the straw buyer and her arranging for bogus documentation to make it appear that the full price had been paid. This is not a case of false advertising, but there's certainly something wrong with it. Most likely, what was done violated state law, but, regardless of that, it was a clear violation of the Realtor® Code of Ethics. Standard of Practice 2-4 specifies :

> Realtors® shall not be parties to the naming of a false
> consideration in any document, unless it be the
> naming of an obviously nominal consideration.

When Nell arranged for the documentation to make it appear that a full price had been paid, this would have constituted the "naming of a false consideration." No doubt, this is something more easily done in some states than others.

The two Case Interpretations (2-10 and 2-11) that deal with naming false considerations are cases where the price was inflated. (It may be equally common that people will try to make it appear that a purchase price was lower than it actually was, because they are trying to keep taxes down.) Nell, too, sought to create an impression that a high price had been paid. Although her reasons were different from the ones in the Case Interpretations, it is clear that she was in violation of Article 2, which prohibits "misrepresentation ... of pertinent facts relating to the property or the transaction."

5

Working with Buyers

The representation of buyers is more complicated than it used to be. In the old days—which really weren't all that long ago—cooperating brokers were subagents of the listing agent. The MLS offer of compensation was based on that understanding. Legally and technically, everyone was working for the seller.

Not everyone understood this. Certainly, a large portion of buyers didn't realize it, and, as a matter of fact, a lot of agents didn't seem to understand it either. The emotional and psychological dynamics between buyers and their agents were no different then than they are now, and more than a few agents were proud that they "fought" for their buyers' interests, even though they were actually subagents of the seller. This all began to change after the Federal Trade Commission conducted extensive studies which showed that buyers generally failed to understand that their agents were legally bound to be working for the seller.

Currently, around the country there is a hodgepodge of laws regarding agency relationships with buyers (and, of course, sellers too). In some states it is clear that the broker/firm is the principal's agent, and if the broker/firm represents both buyer and seller, then it is dual agency. In every case, if there is dual agency, the principals must give informed consent.

Some states don't allow dual agency. Some allow for designated agency, where one agent (i.e., an individual sales or broker associate) in the company represents the buyer, and another agent in the same company represents the seller. But this has different meanings in different states. The disclosure given under Connecticut real estate regulations advises that "A Designated Buyer's Agent and Designated Seller's Agent owe the party for whom they have been appointed undivided fiduciary obligations..." whereas the New York State Disclosure Form for Buyer and Seller states, "A designated sales associate cannot provide the full range of fiduciary duties to the buyer or seller."

This is not the place to attempt to explain all the different agency models, nor is it the place to argue for one over the others. In the discussions that follow we will assume that ultimately it is the broker/ firm that is the agent of the principal, and we will assume, as the Code of Ethics does, that dual agency is a possibility. We make no assumptions about its desirability.

Any discussion of working with buyers will also raise the issue of buyer-broker agreements. These can take a variety of forms. As with agency, this is not the place, nor am I the person, either to describe or to make judgments about the various possibilities. For our purposes here, we will assume that the person working with the buyer is the agent of the buyer, but not necessarily one who is acting pursuant to a buyer-broker agreement that deals with compensation issues.

Not only are there legal and contractual complications with respect to buyer agency, but also, just as with sellers, the Realtor®'s relationship to the buyer may be multifaceted. Buyer agents, like listing agents, often have to fulfill an educational role in dealing with their principals. Buyers read the newspapers selectively too, and they are just as subject to advice and counsel from others who may be quite ignorant as to the realities of the current marketplace.

But buyer agents are called upon to be more than teachers to their clients. They are also likely to be called upon to play the role of psychological counselor, financial advisor, and, let's not forget, crystal ball reader. Buyers can drive agents nuts, and they can provide some of the most rewarding client-agent relationships imaginable. (Indeed, sometimes the same buyer can do both in the same transaction.) Just as the buyer-agent relationship can have its emotional ups and downs, it can present occasions for ethical ups and downs as well. It is the latter that we hope to avoid.

Self-Interested Showing

The market was slow and getting slower. Inventory was high and getting higher. Yet Herb just couldn't find the right place for the Parsons. They had been out looking together on three different occasions, and he had shown them a lot of properties in the South Shore area. All to no avail.

"I just don't know, Herb," John Parson began. Sharon and I love this area, but maybe it isn't the place for us. You've shown us a lot of nice properties, but none of them has had a floor plan that clicks for us. Everything has had a kitchen that seems cut off—separate—from the eating area. Now I understand a lot of people like that. They don't want the dinner guests to look at the clutter, etc., etc. But that's not us. We like everything to be open. In this household the queen happens to be the cook too. She wants to be able to hold court and fix meals at the same time."

"John, I know just what you mean," Herb responded. "I am so glad you have put it so clearly. Wait just a minute while I go get something."

It took Herb just a minute to get what he was looking for from the office "library," and he came back into the conference room holding a floor plan book that covered practically every development in the South Shore area.

"Let me show you two: there's the Ponderosa plan in The Pines development, and the Ambrosia—where do they get these names?—in the Lakeside project. Both would be in your price range, and both have the kind of arrangement you're talking about. The kitchen has a serving counter—you could put three or four barstools there—and opens to a breakfast nook and the family room—right where all the activity takes place."

The Parsons were impressed and delighted. They liked the looks of both, and the bedroom arrangements were just fine. "So, when can we see one?" asked John. "You find us one of these with a view, and I think we'll have a deal."

"Oh, you'd have seen one by now, if there were any on the market. In fact, the last of either of these that has been available was a Ponderosa that closed about six weeks ago." They don't come on very often, but we'll find one. I'll put the word out, and I'll start beating the bushes myself. Count on it!"

Herb was true to his word. He pitched the Parsons at the local "have-want" session (it was fun just to be able to say he had a buyer), let his friends and office-mates know, and started working with the title company to figure out which units were the right model, so that he could send out a mailing. He'd probably have come up with one on his own too, but it turned out not to be necessary.

There it was, six days later, on the MLS hot sheet. A Ponderosa model, with a view—and oh by the way, with a $10,000 bonus to the selling agent! At $575,000 the price seemed a bit high, but the remarks indicated the property was extensively upgraded.

Herb previewed the property immediately, and it was a go. When he called the Parsons they could scarcely contain their excitement. They would be up Saturday morning. "I'm bringing my checkbook," said John.

"*They* were excited?" thought Herb. *He* was ecstatic. He was looking at a handsome commission, his first in a couple of months, *and* the bonus. His broker had even told him that, if he got this deal together, he wouldn't even have to subject the bonus to his regular split. He could have the whole thing!

It was late Friday afternoon when Miko, one of Herb's favorite competitor agents, called. "Herb, I heard your pitch at the have-want session. I think I have what you're looking for. It's an Ambrosia model in Lakeside, not as nicely tricked out as the Ponderosa that came on this week, but get this: It's only going to be $525,000, and it has a better view!

"The owners weren't going to put it on the market until a couple of months from now, but they would show it to your people, if they're really serious. Could you get them up this weekend?"

Herb had never been a standout at school, but he could work with numbers, especially ones with $ signs in front of them. "Miko, I really thank you for calling, but I don't think this weekend will work. I will get together with them and get back to you."

The Parsons loved the Ponderosa. It didn't have quite the view that John had wanted, but the queen had found her kitchen. They couldn't wait to get back to the office to write up an offer. Herb saw no need to confuse the issue by bringing up the property Miko had called about.

It took some time to come up with a number to offer. The Parsons knew it was a slow market. The Ponderosa that had sold six weeks ago closed for $535,000, but it had only a small view. John wasn't going to offer full price, but he didn't want to miss this chance. Finally, he came in at $565,000, and they ultimately settled at $567,500.

The bonus, which Herb hadn't bothered to mention to the Parsons, remained intact.

Everyone was delighted.

Self-Interested Showing: Comments and Analysis

It's pretty easy to make a case against Herb. What would his defense be? "I didn't want to confuse them"? Oh, please. He clearly put his interest ahead of the Parsons'. This is not to say that they would have bought the other, less-expensive one with the better view, had it been shown to them. We've all been surprised at times by the choices our clients make. But it needs to be their choice, not ours.

Most of us are not likely to find ourselves in a situation with facts comparable to those in Herb's case, with such big numbers at stake. But selling agent certainly face enough situations where tempting incentives may be offered. For a good example, see Case Interpretation 1-26.

What is more likely—especially with the current and continuing introduction of nontraditional business models and the "opening" of

MLS systems—is that agents are likely to find that some of the possible showings available come with significantly lower offers of compensation to the selling agent. Some may offer practically no compensation at all. In many cases, these offerings may be less than the buyer's agent is willing to work for. Imagine, for example, that in our scenario, one of the properties offered 3½% to the selling office, and the other offered 1%. There is a fiduciary duty to the buyer; what is an agent to do?

Before addressing the question, let us acknowledge the existence of buyer-broker agreements and the arguments of their proponents. There are many forms of buyer-broker agreements, just as there are many variations of listing agreements. A typical buyer-broker agreement might look something like this: The buyer employs an agent to look for certain types of property, to write offers, to negotiate a sale, and to usher the transaction through closing. As compensation, the buyer will pay x% of the purchase price to his agent. If the seller, or seller's agent, is offering compensation to the buyer's agent, that will be counted as an offset against the x%. (Again, this is not the only kind of buyer-broker arrangement, but it is a common one.)

With an agreement like that, the buyer-broker proponents claim, the agent will not have a self-interested reason not to show properties that offer low compensation. They are right.[11]

Buyer-broker agreements are a great idea. But let's face it: for a variety of reasons, not everyone uses buyer-broker agreements. Probably, most don't. It has yet to become the standard way of doing business in the industry.

So we are back to the original question. You don't have a buyer-broker agreement. You know of one or more properties that fit your client's needs, but some of them offer compensation lower than you are willing to work for. What should you do?

---

[11] Though, in the scenario, even with a buyer-broker agreement, Herb still would have the temptation to which he succumbed.

First (and, really, rather simply), you should try to negotiate with the seller or agent for a higher compensation in the event you bring a successful offer.[12] What you *don't* do is to write an offer and, within the terms of the offer, attempt to change the amount of compensation to the selling agent. That is specifically prohibited by Standard of Practice 16-16:

> Realtors®, acting as subagents or buyer/tenant representatives or brokers, shall not use the terms of an offer to purchase/lease to attempt to modify the listing broker's offer of compensation to subagents or buyer/tenant representatives or brokers nor make the submission of an executed offer to purchase/lease contingent on the listing broker's agreement to modify the offer of compensation.

(For elaboration, see Case Interpretation 16-15.)

If negotiating with the seller or buyer works, great. But, what if it doesn't? Then, you are just going to need to have a discussion with your client. Explain the situation. It is perfectly all right—not a violation of your fiduciary duty—to tell your client that you won't work for free, or for some minimal amount. You'd be surprised; people understand such things. You might want to suggest the buyer-broker concept for those special cases, if not for the entire agency.

Of course, it's possible that none of that would work. You might have a buyer who said something like: "I don't care. That compensation thing is your problem. I just want to be shown whatever properties fit what I am looking for." In that case, you might want to direct them to see the properties on their own. Or maybe you would want to terminate your agency with them. It wouldn't be the end of the world. But what you don't want to do is to deliberately keep them from knowing about those properties, while at the same time occupying a position where you are supposed to put the client's interests first.

---

[12] I don't mean to imply that it would be OK to negotiate directly with the seller if the seller has an agent. You would negotiate with the seller if the seller were unrepresented—a FSBO.

Steering

Having breakfast with her clients before showing didn't really suit Pam's style. There were always those last-minute calls to make and the possibility that someone had called the office to say that, no, she couldn't show their house this morning after all. But, in this case, she was just going to have to trust that the appointments she had made last night were still on and that everything was on track.

Besides, she really liked Rick and Anna. They had hit it off almost from the moment the two of them walked into her office. Imagine— she and Anna had both been high school softball pitchers—and Anna would be delighted to play in the city league that Pam belonged to.

Not only were they nice, they were great buyers too. Rick, with his brand new MBA, had just been promoted and transferred here by the Colinga Company, the town's largest employer. He had an excellent job and excellent credit. Actually, because he and Anna were first-time buyers, with no equity from a previous home, they would probably be buying in a lower price range than would be typical for someone in Rick's salary bracket; but that was OK. He and Anna were just excited about purchasing a first home, and Pam was delighted to be working with well-qualified, noncontingent buyers.

Their first time out had been a good session—Pam learned a lot about them, and they learned a lot about the market. Condos and townhomes were ruled out, even though there were some very nice ones in the price range. When Pam explained that the only alternatives in detached homes would be older, without as much square footage, that was all right. "Pam," Rick explained, "the company will probably keep me here at least three years, maybe five. Now that I've finished my MBA, we want to start a family. Having a yard is really important to us. If the house is a little small and a bit older, that's OK with us. You should see where we grew up!"

So, they looked at four homes that Tuesday afternoon: one in the Silver Springs tract, one in El Dorado, and two in Grande Vista. All of them were fine, but none was quite the right one. Today, Thursday,

Pam had four more to show them; and she gave them brief descriptions before the waiter came to take their order.

As soon as the waiter left, Rick began. "Pam, we like you a lot, and we really appreciate the work you are doing; but we are a little uneasy that something not right is going on.

"We know that our financial situation doesn't buy much, even in this part of California, and that there's not a lot to look at in our price range. Still, you're not showing us everything.

In particular, you haven't shown us anything in the Del Rio area, and you haven't planned to show us anything today. Anna picked up one of those real estate magazines yesterday, and she did some driving around. She found out that there are some Del Rio homes available that are in our price range. One of them is even a listing from your office. (Pam knew it well.) But you aren't showing us anything there. Does it have something to do with us being Mexican-Americans? What's going on?"

It seemed like the 15-second silence lasted about an hour, with Pam looking down the whole time. Then, she lifted her head and began, "You are absolutely right, and I am so sorry if I have offended you. Believe me; I have only had your interest at heart.

"All the places we have looked at are in neighborhoods where I know you would be welcomed and you would be comfortable. I don't think that would be true in the Del Rio tract. Del Rio was actually the first real development in this town. Most of the people who moved into it worked at the plant. Most of them still do, though a good number have already retired.

"It's a pretty tight community, and, frankly—I just don't know any other way to say this—it's a redneck community. I mean, they even have a Minuteman chapter in that neighborhood. (She didn't mention that the next-door neighbor to the office listing was the leader of the chapter.)

"I just didn't think it was the right place for you."

Now it was Rick and Anna's turn to be silent. Finally, Anna spoke. "Pam, we do understand, and believe me, we appreciate your concern for us. But let *us* be the ones to deal with the problem, if there is a problem. Goodness knows, we've done it before. Do you know that Rick was the only Latino in the MBA program? Even in a college town, some people acted like it was a mistake that he was there, or that there must have been some sort of affirmative action thing going on.

"Anyway, Pam, just show us those houses too. We'll deal with whatever comes up."

Wouldn't you know it? Pam showed them the Del Rio houses; and they fell in love with the one that was an office listing. Pam and the listing agent presented the offer that evening. It was full price and clean as could be.

Naturally, there was no discussion of Rick and Anna's ethnicity, though, of course, Pam touted the fact that Rick was with the company and appeared to be on a junior management fast track. The seller liked that a lot. He thought that some of his good-old-boy friends would get a kick out of saying that they were in a "management neighborhood" now.

Pam was just pulling into the driveway, having returned from Rick and Anna's hotel, where they confirmed receipt of the seller's acceptance, and then had a celebratory drink in the lounge. What a roller coaster day! She was elated, yet still apprehensive.

The cell phone rang. A message was being forwarded from her office voicemail: "You'd better listen real good, real estate lady. You tell them beaners they'd better change their minds. Tell them they can just go back across the river where they belong. We don't want their kind here; and they sure as hell ain't gonna want to be here either."

"Uh-oh," she thought, "it's already beginning."

Steering: Comments and Analysis

In April 2006 the National Fair Housing Alliance (NFHA) released a report that compiled 26,092 documented complaints of housing discrimination in 2005. The NFHA believes 99% of acts of housing discrimination go unreported. It estimates there are about 3.7 million instances each year.

Real estate columnist Kenneth Harney reported that NFHA:

> conducted 'paired sales tests' in 12 metropolitan areas between early 2003 and mid-2005. The tests involved whites, Latinos and African-Americans posing as prospective home buyers in repeat visits to realty brokerage firms to detect any patterns of differential treatment by agents.

> In each paired investigation, there was a team of testers, one white and one either African-American or Latino. Two teams of testers contacted the same real estate sales office. In all cases, the teams were assigned similar information about housing needs, financial qualifications and employment history. In every instance, the African-American or Latino teams were slightly more qualified than the white teams in terms of income, downpayment ability, outstanding debt loads and length of employment tenure.

> According to the report, "almost 20 percent of the time, African American and Latino testers were refused appointments or offered very limited service" in comparison with white testers. Whites were shown more homes—a total of 1,144 or 8 homes per test, while minority testers were shown 732 homes in total, an average of 5 homes per test.[13]

In a particularly egregious instance in Chicago, the NFHA report stated: "Against her own economic interest, one real estate agent told a

---

[13] Kenneth Harney, "Fair Housing Study Blasts Realty Agents for Alleged 'Steering' and Racial Discrimination," *Realty Times*, April 10, 2006.

potential African-American home buyer that he should rent rather than buy, although his financial profile was stronger than his white counterpart's. He was shown no units—the white home seeker working with the same agent saw 21 units."

Steering—the practice of showing buyers only a selected subset of available properties on the basis of factors such as race or religion—is against the law. It is also a violation of Article 10 of the Realtor® Code of Ethics:

> Realtors® shall not deny equal professional services to any person for reasons of race, color, religion, sex, handicap, familial status, or national origin. Realtors® shall not be parties to any plan or agreement to discriminate against a person or persons on the basis of race, color, sex, handicap, familial status, or national origin.

When two parties are looking for a similar type of property, and one person sees eight properties and the other, better-qualified party sees only five, that is a denial of equal professional services. If it is done on the basis of race, it is both unethical and illegal.

It may sound odd to say, but discrimination in the form of steering can be well-intentioned. Pam, in our story, bore no malice toward Rick and Anna. She didn't want to harm them. Quite to the contrary, she was trying to look out for their interests—at least what she perceived to be their interests. She might even have been right about that; but the point is: It is *not* the agent's call. 2006 NAR president, Thomas Stevens, has nicely stated the downside of even well-intentioned steering:

> Many associates identified as having engaged in steering felt they were doing a service to buyers by providing unasked-for advice. Others no doubt thought they were helping protect their community's property values. *But that line of thinking is insidious, because when we think of and speak of factors such as race, ethnicity, and national origin as having a* material impact *on values, we make it so.* We also break the

law and violate Article 10 of the Realtor® Code of Ethics. *[my emphasis]* [14]

Many, probably most, good sales agents want everything to go well for their clients. They want them to have good experiences. They may even see it as their job to protect their clients from stress and tension. And those are good feelings to have. But, sometimes, they may not be the right feelings. Sometimes, the ethical thing to do may be just to let the chips fall where they may.

A Different Kind of Dual Agency

"Barry, you know that my relocation company picked you to work with me—and that's just fine with me; they're picking up the tab—but I'm still interested in knowing more about your company and how you operate. You know, it's the only company our relo people will work with, as long as there's one in the area of the transfer."

"I'm glad you asked, Antonio, because I never get tired of telling buyers about this. It just makes so much sense. Buyers Only Realty is what is known as an exclusive buyers' agency. We work only with buyers. We have no listings. Now, we're not the only company that operates this way, but we're one of the largest, if not *the* largest."

"Well, I can attest to that. I think I've seen three of your offices just driving in from the airport and driving around town a little bit."

"That doesn't surprise me," Barry responded; "our broker has sixteen branch offices. He pretty well has the city and the outlying areas covered. But let me get back to the concept. You see, it's all about representation. We represent you and you only. We don't represent any sellers, so you never have to worry that we're going to get into a dual-agency situation. And, of course, that happens all the time with traditional companies. If you call on a sign or an ad for a property for sale, who are you going to get? Someone who is working for the seller.

---

[14] Thomas Stevens, "Stevens Report," *Realtor® Magazine Online*, July 1, 2006.

But, when you use us, you let us do the calling and the inquiring, and ultimately the negotiating, and *you* are the one who is being represented."

Barry went on at some length, and Antonio was impressed; but then came the not-so-good news.

"Of course, even though I am 100% on your side, Antonio, that doesn't mean I can change the market. I'm sure you've read what is going on around here."

He had.

"It's pretty slim pickings for a buyer right now. The inventory of homes for sale is just about at a record low, and the sellers are feeling pretty cocky about it. We've even begun to see multiple offers, and occasionally sales above the listing price.

"So, realize, I can't tell you that you're going to be able to steal something, or even that you can buy at the low end of market price, but I do guarantee exclusive representation for you, and that we'll get something at the lowest price possible. I'm not going to be working for the seller!"

Barry was right about the low inventory. Only four on the MLS were even remotely promising, and two of them were further down the peninsula than Antonio wanted to travel. None of them fit. Next they tried the FSBOs. Again, there were only three that had any potential; and each of them was a no-go also.

Antonio came back two weeks later, only to experience similar results. It was frustrating and discouraging. No wonder, then, that he would make a special trip over in response to Barry's call that there was a new listing that sounded just right. The price, $580,000 was at about the very high end of Antonio's capability, and more than he had wanted to spend, but the market was what the market was.

"Barry, my friend," Ron, the listing agent began, "we've known each other too long for me to blow smoke at you. Listen, this is the truth, and I want you to know it. I could tell your client liked the property, and I would bet you are just about to sit down to write an offer..."

He was absolutely right. They had looked at the property about a half hour ago. A quick phone call to Antonio's wife, and it was a go.

"... but you have to know that there's another offer coming in. In fact, it's from Pam what's-her-name in your Peninsula office. I don't think you know her, but she's a good agent, and she says her buyer is really serious. All I'm saying, buddy, is tell your buyer to take his best shot."

It was a difficult conversation. Where Antonio came from, he wasn't used to prices like these, and he certainly had never experienced market conditions like these. Finally, though, he came around. His offer was full price.

The next morning, Barry was astounded. "What do you mean we didn't get it? Was the other offer *over* list price? How come we didn't even get a counteroffer? I can't believe this!"

"Barry, you know I can't say what the price was," Ron responded, "and you'll see it in MLS soon enough anyway. As to a counter—my seller just didn't want to get into that sort of thing. He didn't want a bidding war. He was happy with the price he received. I'm sorry. I tried to help you as best I could."

Naturally, Barry was puzzled a few weeks later when the MLS showed that the property had sold for $578,000—not even full price. Not that he was going to tell Antonio. Things had pretty well deteriorated on that front. Antonio had lost confidence in him, so the relo company assigned him to another agent in a different office. Barry didn't even bother to call Ron. He just decided to let it go.

It was about a month later that Janet, Barry's broker, called him into her office. "Remember that relo buyer you had—the one who lost out on the multiple-offer situation?"

How could he forget?

"Well, I've just had a call from his lawyer. It seems that the person who beat him out works for the same company. Wouldn't you know it: They have become acquainted, and naturally, the subject of the property came up. The reason the other buyer got the property at the lower price was that his agent, Pam Sellers, from our Peninsula office, offered to cut her commission by $5,000 to the seller, without the buyer having to make up for it. So the seller netted more, even though the price was lower.

"This lawyer says that Buyers Only did a disservice to his client, that our company put him at a disadvantage and helped a competing buyer get the property, that we were dual agents in this transaction, and we didn't even let him know it, much less get his consent.

"He wants to know what we are going to do about it. Any suggestions?"

A Different Kind of Dual Agency: Comments and Analysis

Traditionally, dual agency occurs when the same agent represents both the buyer and the seller. Intuitively, when we think of the *same agent* we are liable to mean the *same person*. But, as most of us know by now, that is not generally deemed to be the case. Rather, the agent is the broker or the firm. To be sure, no one talks that way. People say, "My agent was Janice," not "My agent was the Johnston Company," or the like. Nonetheless, the reality is that the company/broker is the agent, and we need to think that way.

The difficulty in thinking rightly about dual agency is compounded by increasing consolidation and the emergence of multi-office mega companies. Suppose that Down Home Realty is a single-office, eight-person brokerage and that Megan has the listing and Bob has the buyer. In that situation, with one broker-manager, and an atmosphere where everyone pretty much knows what everyone else is doing, it may not seem such a fiction to think that Down Home is the agent and that there is dual agency with all its potential for conflict.

On the other hand, imagine this: MegaRealty is an 1100-agent company with 15 offices spread over three counties.[15] Most of the agents

---

[15] It is not that MegaRealty is a franchise, and that the different offices are independently owned. MegaRealty is one company, under a single ownership.

don't even know all the people in their own offices, much less the others throughout the company. Now, here, when an agent from the MegaRealty office in Quartz City, about 30 miles away, brings a buyer to a listing of an agent he's never met in the Canyon Creek office, it just doesn't feel like dual agency. But it is.

Our scenario reminds us of the fact that a multiple-office firm is going to be considered as a single agent. It also introduces us to a relatively new, but emerging, consideration with respect to real estate brokerages and agency: Dual-agency conflicts may not be confined to cases where the apparent conflicting interests are those of a buyer and a seller.

For those who think that dual agency is a problem, the nature of the problem is this: How can one agent represent parties who have conflicting interests? But, if that's the issue, then we need to be aware that buyers and sellers in a given transaction are not the only ones who may have conflicting interests. As our scenario has shown, it is quite possible for two (or more) different buyers to have conflicting interests. Namely, they may all want the same house.

I'm not making this up. In 2007 the Montana State Supreme Court ruled that, under Montana state law, a buyer agent breaches his obligation to a buyer when that agent simultaneously represents more than one buyer.[16] In the Montana case, both buyers were represented by the same individual. Moreover, it was not characterized as "dual agency," because Montana law specifically defines *dual agency* as representing both a seller and a buyer.

To be sure, agency law differs from state to state, and different conclusions might be reached in different states, even if the facts were similar.

Standard of Practice 1-5 addresses the dual agency issue this way:

> Realtors® may represent the seller/landlord and buyer/
> tenant in the same transaction only after full disclosure to
> and with informed consent of both parties.

---

[16] *Amador F. Zuazua v. Tom and Corl Tibbles, individually and dba Coldwell Banker Gateway Realty, and Patty Stone* The Montana Court was answering a question put to it by a Federal Court in which the case was being heard.

This is a good thing. But the Code has not yet addressed the issue of representing competing buyers or competing sellers. It would probably be desirable to begin developing some professional ethics standards and guidelines for those situations.

There's no question that it's an ethical issue. Try some Golden Rule thinking here. Wouldn't you want to know if your agent were representing someone who is competing with you? Don't you think you should have to give your consent for that? We probably have no trouble seeing the problem if we think of a situation where the agent is the same person. But we need to remember that agency issues apply to the firm, not just the individuals.

One final note: This discussion has taken place primarily in the context of competing buyers. But the issues are the same when it comes to sellers who are competing with each other. In fact, the situation where the same *person* is the agent for competing sellers is much more likely to occur. It happens to successful "farmers" all the time.

6

Negotiations

It's hard to say exactly when negotiations start in a real estate transaction. Perhaps the line should be drawn at the time an offer is presented. But if that is to be the case, then we need to label and recognize as "pre-negotiations" all those queries and comments that commonly precede a written offer. We've all heard them: "Where did your seller get that price?" "Are your people familiar with the comps?" "My buyer is ready to move, and he doesn't want to fool around." And on and on.

Ad campaigns by Realtor® associations, as well as advertising by individual Realtors®, frequently refer to negotiating ability. Sellers are told that they want to have a strong negotiator on their side, and FSBOs are warned that they don't want to try to sell without a professional negotiating on their behalf. It can be a powerful appeal.

Yet the sense in which an agent acts as a negotiator is a curious one. Unlike union-management negotiators or negotiators at diplomatic talks, agents don't work out a deal with their counterparts and then come back to their principals for ratification. It is not the agent who makes the proposals or crafts the responses; it is the principal. What the agent does, primarily, is to advise on the proposals and counterproposals that the principal will make.

The agent may argue or advocate to the other principal for his own principal's position, but even this function is typically limited. It may be standard fare for a buyer's agent to pitch his client's original offer.[17] But it is certainly not common for the seller's agent to present a counteroffer in the same manner. (It happens, and it makes good sense; but it is pretty unusual.) And, if there are further rounds of

---

[17] Even this, in the era of fax machines and pdf files, is becoming more of a rarity.

counteroffers, it would be highly unlikely that they would be person-ally presented and argued for by the respective agents.

So, whom do agents negotiate with? Generally, other agents. While, as noted, it would be pretty unusual for a listing agent to present a counteroffer to a buyer, it is very common for the listing agent to have jawboned with the buyer's agent about the terms of the counter—for them to have talked about everything from the price and length of escrow to the reason why it is important that the chandelier stay with the property.

When agents enter into these kinds of discussions, they need to be careful about crossing over ethical lines. We know that we have a fiduciary duty to act in our client's interest, but it is important to watch out that we don't substitute what we think the client should do for what it is that the client really wants.[18]

In the course of agent-to-agent discussions, it is also very easy to lose track of the obligation not to reveal confidential information about our clients. A commonly asked question by buyers' representatives is, "What is the seller's motivation?" Often, the answer to this may contain confidential information that not only does the seller wish to keep private, but also that may be used to the seller's disadvantage in negotiating.

Standard of Practice 1-9 spells out in some detail the obligations agents have with respect to confidential information:

> The obligation of REALTORS® to preserve confidential information (as defined by state law) provided by their clients in the course of any agency relationship or non-agency relationship recognized by law continues after termination of agency relationships or any non-agency relationships recognized by law. REALTORS® shall not

---

[18] This needs to be distinguished from our earlier remarks about the agent's role in educating the client. If the client says he wants $250,000 for the property, and we know it is worth $275,000, we need to make him aware of that.

knowingly, during or following the termination of professional relationships with their clients:

1) reveal confidential information of clients; or

2) use confidential information of clients to the disadvantage of clients; or

3) use confidential information of clients for the REALTOR®'s advantage or the advantage of third parties unless:

    a) clients consent after full disclosure; or

    b) REALTORS® are required by court order; or

    c) it is the intention of a client to commit a crime and the information is necessary to prevent the crime; or

    d) it is necessary to defend a REALTOR® or the REALTOR®'s employees or ASSOCIATEs against an accusation of wrongful conduct.

Information concerning latent material defects is not considered confidential information under this Code of Ethics.

Realtors® especially need to be aware of the obligation not to reveal confidential information or to use it to the advantage of third parties not only during, but also "following the termination of professional relationships with their clients." Thus, for example, even after the listing has expired, the former listing agent is obliged to honor the seller's confidences.

One aspect of Standard of Practice 1-9 is potentially confusing. The Standard begins by referring to "confidential information (as defined by state law) ...." We should not take this parenthetical qualifying phrase as limiting the application of the Standard.[19] Not only is it unlikely that many Realtors® will know how their state law defines *confidential information*, but it is also the case that this term is not defined by law in every state. *Confidential information* may be more like *procuring cause*. We may not be able to find a precise definition for it.

[19] I am indebted to Susie Kater, Counsel for the California Association of Realtors®, for this insight.

At best, we can see applications in various cases and precedents, and we may have to make our own judgments as to whether it applies in a particular circumstance.

With respect to the strictures of Standard of Practice 1-9, we should construe it broadly. Suppose, for example, that your client has told you, "We have filed for divorce, but I want that kept confidential. I don't want anybody to know about it." Well, if they have filed in court, it is already public knowledge in the sense that the information is available to the public. Nonetheless, for your purposes, it is confidential, and you are not to speak of it to anyone—especially the agent on the other side of the transaction.

In this respect, defining *confidential information* becomes rather easy. If the client wants something to be kept confidential, then, unless it falls within specified exceptions[20], you should treat it as such.

Agents negotiate for their clients, often with great effectiveness, in their conversations with other agents. But, in their zeal to secure a favorable deal for those they represent, they need to be careful that they do not inadvertently undermine the interests they are meant to serve.

Making the Deal

"So, what's it going to take?" Valerie asked, as she slowly poured another beer into Scott's outstretched mug. "He can't *really* be stuck on that price, can he?"

"I love it when we play these games," Scott laughed, "and I suppose your guy's $380,000 was his last best offer, right?"

Scott and Valerie were with different companies, but they had known each other for years. They had done transactions with each other before, but not all that many. Indeed, they had both remarked how

---

[20] See, for example, those specified in Standard of Practice 1-9. There also may be other exceptions specified by law.

odd it seemed that, even though they were active agents in a town of just under 35,000, they really hadn't done a lot of business with each other. But they had talked about plenty of deals and situations that both they and their colleagues had been involved in. It would be fair to say that they knew how each other thought.

The occasion of today's over-a-pitcher-of-beer conversation was the offer that Valerie had just presented to Scott's client. The principals in this situation made for a classic match-up. Scott's seller was one of those who consistently listed high because, "I can always come down." Valerie's buyer was a habitual low-baller. "There's no harm in trying, and, besides, sometimes I get pleasantly surprised."

Scott's client, though, had declined even to give a counter-offer. As he told, Scott, "I'd just be competing with myself."

Both Valerie and Scott knew market values well—they'd been around and they were pros—and they wished their clients would just take their advice, forget about this little buyer-seller dance, and get on with realistic business. But that wasn't happening, at least not yet.

Now it was Valerie's turn. "Scott, I know somebody was smoking something illegal when that $525,000 price was set. Tell me he's ready to come down and be realistic. For crying out loud, not even a counter!"

"Well, I'm not going to blow smoke at you, Val. Of course, that's an unreal price, and he knows it. But, look, I really don't know exactly what he'll take, but I do know this: he needs this sale, and he's told me the why and wherefore. He went and committed himself to a noncontingent purchase on another property—it was out of state, and I had nothing to do with it. Anyway, he thought he had proceeds coming out of an inheritance, but then one of the other heirs had a problem, and now that's all tangled up with the lawyers. His only other source of funds would be the sale of this property.

"I've gone over the costs with him, and he's going to need about $450,000 out of this sale in order to close the other one—otherwise, he's going to lose a pretty sizeable deposit. But don't you let on to him that you know any of this. He's really embarrassed about the pickle he's got himself in, and he doesn't want anyone to know.

"Val, you and I both know that $450,000 would be a decent price for that property."

"I'm sure not going to argue with you about that, Scott, but I don't know if we can do it. I know that my guy will go to $435,000—he told me so. But $450,000? I just don't know."

"Val, you get your guy to come in at $435,000, and I'll really push on my end. He can scrape up a few more bucks from somewhere else—it doesn't all have to come out of this deal—and I'll keep reminding him of what he stands to lose."

Valerie did her part, but Scott's client responded at $460,000. It turned out that Scott was right, though. After a number of discussions, both agent-to-principal and agent-to-agent, they went into contract at $440,000. Scott's client got $5,000 from another source, and Scott and Valerie contributed $2,500 each from their commissions.

They told their clients that they were deal-makers, and their clients loved it.

Making the Deal: Comments and Analysis

This sort of thing happens all the time. But it shouldn't.

Telling others that a seller will take less than the listed price—without specific authorization to do so—is probably the classic, most-often-committed violation of the Realtor® Code of Ethics. Telling a seller, or a seller's representative, that your buyer is willing to pay more than he has offered is something that probably doesn't happen as often, but, for a buyer's agent, it is the counterpart of the classic listing agent violation.

When Scott divulged his seller's situation and need to sell, he simply compounded his violation of Article 1, the article that requires Realtors® to "protect and promote the interests of their client." Case

Interpretation 1-1 provides an instructive example on this point.

Having said all that, we really should look at the behavior of the agents a little more deeply, indeed, sympathetically.

These are not what we would call *bad people*. Nor, I suspect, are most of the agents who divulge their clients' motives and likely price points.

Valerie wasn't out to see her client get gouged, and Scott was trying to accomplish something that he perceived to be in his client's best interests. Moreover, it is trite, and wrong, to say that the only thing the Realtors® were interested in was getting a commission. *Of course*, they wanted to receive a commission. But the main thing was that they were trying to put a deal together—one that would meet their clients' needs. Sure, commissions come from doing that, but that doesn't demonstrate uncaring, selfish interests on part of the agents.

For the sake of argument, let's stipulate that there was no harm here and that there was no bad intent on the part of the agents. So, someone might say, "Why, then, should we get all cranked up about violating the Code?"

A question like this is really a question as to why we should have ethics codes at all—be they professional or not. And the answer is this:

Codes, such as the Realtor® Code of Ethics, set forth principles of behavior for us to follow. They are not *guarantees* that, if followed, results will always be great; nor is it the case that not following them will always result in harm. But it is true that if we get in the habit of following them, things will generally be better for all involved. Moreover, because the underlying principle of such codes is *respect for others*, if we follow them, people will know they have been treated with respect, and that in itself is no small matter.

When we take it upon ourselves to depart from the Code, as in these violations of Article 1, we substitute our judgment for that of our clients. (Note: Substituting our judgment is not the same as educating them.) When we substitute our judgment, we treat them in a way that we wouldn't want to be treated ourselves. And that is not a good thing, even if the deal gets done.

The Perfect Buyers

Ali had not expected the listing appointment to take nearly this long. But, then, he really should have known. His family had known the Kellers for years. Their kids used to babysit Ali and his brother. So when Martha Keller called and told him she was ready to list her house, he figured it would be a slam dunk, quick and easy appointment. And it was, as far as her accepting his price suggestion and the terms of the listing. But he hadn't counted on—although he should have—the nostalgia tour of the house, the talk about how he used to help her late husband, Earl, with his beloved garden, how they had raised their family there, etc., etc., etc.

Ali was recounting the appointment story to his good friend and fellow Realtor®, Nathan. They worked for different companies, but their friendship far transcended any business rivalries they might have had. They were a lot closer to each other than to anyone in either of their respective offices.

"So here we were," Ali went on, "going over her life, her kids' lives, my family's life, my childhood .... She just wouldn't stop. It got to the point that I was afraid to mention any feature of the house or grounds, because that would trigger another story. Anyway, I've got the listing, and I think $650,000 is a damn good price. It's not a giveaway, but it does account for all the work that needs to be done." Nathan concurred with no reservations.

"The frustrating thing," Ali went on, "is that I really can't market this the way I would like to. I mean it is, if not a fixer, at least something with a lot more potential than its current state. I'd like to flat-out pitch it as a money-maker. You know, where someone could come in and tear out those trees to get the view, plow under that old garden and re-landscape the yard, get rid of that silly 'garden room' enclosure and open it up to the patio, and on and on.

"But she would have a cow if she saw that I had advertised it like that. Not only does she think everything is just perfect the way she and Earl did it, but she thinks someone else is going to come in and think so too. She thinks someone will want to raise a family and live there forty years just the way they did, all enclosed by the trees and everything.

"And what's really crazy, Nate, is this: She's not even going to be around to know about it. I mean, to hear her talk she's going to be visiting with the buyers and bringing them cookies every day; but, as a matter of fact, as soon as this is sold, she's moving up north to live in a retirement home close to her oldest son. To tell the truth, I wish she'd move up there now, so I could go ahead and market this the way it should be marketed."

It was just two days later that Nathan was sitting in the conference room with Craig, one of his best investor clients. "I'm telling you, Craig, this one is a winner."

"You don't have to tell me again, Nathan. Now that I've seen it, I am totally convinced. Let's write it up."

"OK, great, but let me go over a couple of things with you first. One is that the word is another offer is coming in. Ali told me that he hasn't actually received it yet, but another agent told him to expect something by this afternoon.

"The other is that we want to employ a special strategy here. If we do it right, I think we'll really strengthen your hand."

"Well, you know me, Nathan. If another offer comes in, so be it. You know I won't do a bidding war; I'll just offer what makes sense to me and that's that. But what is this strategy idea?"

"Craig," Nathan almost whispered, "I know something about the owner and what her 'hot button' is liable to be. She's got a lot of emotional attachment to this house, and she wants the buyer to have the same. So let's satisfy her. I'm going to draft a letter for you and Cindy to sign, which I will then present to her along with the offer. Maybe I'll even read it aloud. It will rave about how this is your dream home and the perfect place to raise your family. We'll go on about how the garden reminds you of your childhood home and how you'll want to restore it and work it in. Yadda yadda yadda. We'll lay it on thick; and then I'll say the same kind of stuff about the two of you who want to live there forever. I guarantee it will help your offer."

Nathan was right, of course. Even though the other offer was $640,000, she took Craig and Cindy's offer of $635,000 because she was so thrilled that they were the perfect buyers for the home where she and Earl had raised their family.

Martha moved away almost immediately after the sale closed. She passed away less than a year later. She never did learn that Craig and his partners tore out the trees and garden, re-landscaped, modernized the house, and flipped it for a handsome profit within six months. Nathan was the listing agent, and Ali brought the buyer.

The Perfect Buyers: Comments and Analysis

Many agents are taught, and rightly so, to portray their buyers in a favorable light to the sellers when they are presenting an offer. This is often a useful thing to do in residential sales, where sellers may sometimes be more influenced by intangibles than sellers of commercial or investment properties might be.

Puffing the buyers has become something of a lost art form in an era when offers are more likely to come over the fax machine or appear in an electronic in-box, having just arrived from somewhere in cyberspace. It is still not entirely unheard of, though, to receive some written story about and/or by the buyers when one receives an offer in these ways. And, interestingly, it can still be effective.

Making a buyer appear attractive to a seller is one thing; outright deception is another. Article 1 of the Realtor® Code of Ethics clearly obligates Realtors® to treat "all parties honestly." So, of course, does everyday ethics. To be sure, Nathan was trying to promote his own clients' interests, but even the exercise of fiduciary duty does not provide a waiver from the obligation to be honest.

Some agents don't get this. They get so wrapped up in their desire, and duty, to serve their clients' interests that they forget that the duty is limited by other ethical constraints. Probably, this is most likely to happen when an agent seeks to make his buyer appear to be stronger financially than he really is. Or there may be an attempt to try to hide or gloss over some unstated contingency that could cause problems down the line.

Dishonesty about a buyer's finances or ability to buy is likely to be uncovered before any damage is done—likely, but not always. In the case of Nathan's story, the seller might have found out after escrow, but, as it turned out, she never did. Did that make it ok, then? Of course, not.

Some might want to object that all this makes a mountain out of a molehill. "It's stupid for her to have all those sentimental attachments and to be so exercised about who the buyers were going to be. It's just a house after all. She needed to get a grip on the fact that after it was sold, it was no longer hers, and that's that."

That is all well and good to say, but people's emotions and attachments are what they are. Even if we think they are totally irrational, it doesn't give us the right to be dishonest with them. Besides, what about that other buyer whose offer was not accepted, because of the deception?

Finally, it's relevant to ask, "What about the listing agent's role in all of this?" There are two questions to be asked: (1) Did he wrongly divulge confidential information? (2) Did he knowingly go along with the misrepresentation of the buyers?

The way Ali talked about his seller may not have been very nice, but there doesn't seem to be any reason to think that he was passing on confidential information. As far as we know, she didn't tell him that her nostalgia was confidential. If anything, you get the idea that she would have been pleased if his advertising could have conveyed her emotional attachment to the property.

Nor do we have any knowledge that Ali knew the story about the buyers was a fabrication. If he did, then he certainly should have told her so. A more likely issue is that, being good friends with Nathan, he very well might have showed favoritism to that offer. Typically, we think of favoritism being shown when the offer is from the listing agent himself or from the same office (see Case Interpretation 1-29); but it isn't unusual—though it can be unethical—to bias a seller toward an offer that is brought by a friend or good acquaintance. We need always to remember that the seller's interest is primary.

Shopping the Offer[21]

The Walling listing had been such a source of frustration to Ellen. It was as if the market just came to a screeching halt the day after she listed it. And it was a good listing, too. It was well-priced at $325,000— at least it seemed so the day she listed it. The property presented itself well; the location, right at the edge of the forest, was dynamite; and even her sellers were wonderful. But, here it was, five months later, and still no offers.

Oh, there had been plenty of activity (which was a good part of the reason there had been no price reduction): the home was shown regularly, and she had even engaged in those "pre-negotiation" rituals ("Aren't you priced a little high?" "Are your sellers not motivated?" "Where did you get that number, anyway?" etc.) with a couple of other agents—both of whom were friends, by the way—but, still, no offers had been written.

So it was no wonder that both Ellen and Ted Walling (Alice Walling was out of town) were excited when Lisa called to say she had an offer to present. Lisa was a friend, too, and a darn good agent, even if she did work for another firm.

"I'm sorry this is not as high an offer as you were looking for," Lisa said after they had gone through the details of price and terms, "but I really think this is the best the Collinses can do. They love your home, and they would move into it tomorrow if they could. But they just can't get here sooner than his three-month transfer date. Please, please give their offer every consideration."

---

[21] A version of this appeared online in *RealtyTimes*, September 15, 2006.

"You know, Ellen," Ted Walling began as soon as Lisa left, "Alice and I had certainly hoped to do better than this $275,000."

"I know, Ted, and I still think we can achieve the kind of price we have set ..."

"Now, now, just a minute. Let me finish. Alice and I have talked about this, and of course we'll have to verify with her when she gets back tomorrow night, but I think we are at the point where we might accept this. Frankly, when we decided to sell, we were ready to sell. This dragging on for months and months has been emotionally hard on us. Actually, though I don't like the idea of going as low as two-seventy-five, the ninety days is almost worse. We just want to be done with this."

"Isn't that the way it always is?" Ellen thought to herself. You never really knew what was going on in sellers' minds until they had an offer in front of them. But she didn't want them to sell themselves short.

"All right, Ted, I understand; but let me suggest something. The Collinses have given you forty-eight hours to respond, knowing that Alice won't be back until tomorrow. Maybe we can get you a better offer before that time is up.

"You know that I have had conversations with both Terrell Hampton and Larry Knowles about their clients who were interested in your property. Well, I know for a fact that their buyers haven't purchased anything yet, so maybe we should put something in front of them."

"I don't understand."

"Well, Ted, with your permission of course, I could go to those agents and let them know what you are considering accepting. I would suggest to them that their clients might try bettering the offer you have before you—no guarantees, of course. Doing that could quite likely elicit an offer from one or both of them. It's not going to get you the $325,000 we had been hoping for; but you might do better than what you are looking at now."

"Is that legal?"

"Absolutely, Ted, you know I wouldn't suggest it if it were not."

"OK, then, Ellen. You go ahead and see what you can do. We know you're looking out for us."

And it worked. Terrell's buyer came in with an offer of $280,000 and a thirty-day escrow period. Larry's, unable to offer a shorter escrow, sought to make up for that by offering $285,000—a full $10,000 over the offer he had been told about.

What a change! Five months of doldrums, and now this. Ellen, Ted, and Alice sat around the table grinning at each other, all of them long over the $325,000 price by now. It was a good thing Ellen was still maintaining some of her professional composure, because Ted and Alice were almost giddy.

"Feast or famine, I guess. We have to hand it to you, Ellen You sure knew what to do," Ted enthused, "but what do we do now? How do we handle this situation?"

"You have a number of options, Ted and Alice. Let me lay them out for you." Ellen went on to explain that they could choose to accept one of the offers as it stood, or they could counter to one while rejecting the others, or they could actually choose the procedure of countering to more than one.

It was more surprising to Ellen than it was to Ted that Alice spoke up, totally on top of the situation. "Well, I think we ought to make counteroffers to all of them, if Ellen says there is a way to do that. We all know that everybody can always do a little bit better than what they offer the first time around. And while we're not going to get what we thought we would, I think we should try to do a little better than these first offers."

After some discussion, they wrote three counteroffers. They asked Terrell's buyer to come up from $280,000 to $285,000. To the other two, because they wanted longer escrow periods, they asked for more— $290,000—but they asked both of them to shorten the time to sixty days.

Ellen prepared the counteroffers on the state form that included a seller-protection procedure, which prevented them from being overobligated if more than one party accepted. She then delivered the counteroffers to each agent respectively. Of course, each one wanted to know what was going on; and she told each one of the other offers and how they were handling the situation.

Sometimes things just don't work out the way you hoped they would.

Lisa's client was furious. He had never heard of such a thing. It seemed both illegal and immoral. (She did not think it would be wise to try to correct him.) And, even though he might have worked with this counteroffer in a straightforward situation, he didn't want to have anything more to do with these people or this property.

The other two had somewhat similar reactions. They both told their agents they didn't want to get into a bidding war.

The Walling listing expired at the end of the 120-day listing period. There had been no further offers, even though they had lowered the price to $305,000.

Shopping the Offer: Comments and Analysis[22]

"Shopping an offer" refers to the practice of informing other potential buyers, or their agents, of the price and/or terms of an offer that has been made on one's own listing. Ellen was shopping the offer that had been brought by Lisa.

At the November 2004 meetings of the National Association of Realtors®, the topic of shopping offers became the subject of an intense debate. A proposal had been made requiring that buyers be notified that their offers might be shopped. Specifically, a new Standard of Practice was proposed:

---

[22] Versions of parts of this discussion appeared in *Realty Times*, December 12, 2004, and February 2, 2006.

> Realtors® assisting purchasers in formulating purchase
> offers shall advise those purchasers that the existence,
> terms and conditions of any offer they make may
> potentially be disclosed to other purchasers by sellers or
> by sellers representatives except where such disclosure is
> prohibited by law or regulation.

The proposal provoked heated discussion, the focus of which was more on the practice of shopping offers itself than it was on the proposal that the practice be disclosed.

Some made the argument that shopping offers ought not to be done, perhaps not even allowed, because it is unproductive. This is sometimes true. Certainly, in the case of the Walling listing, Ellen's offer-shopping backfired, as can certainly happen. Buyers can easily be turned off when they know it is happening, and, as happened with the Wallings, all the buyers may withdraw. In light of that possibility, the decision to shop an offer is a judgment call, just like most business decisions.

Others who engaged in the NAR debate simply found the practice of shopping offers to be distasteful, a bit unseemly; and they objected to it strongly because of that. "Doing that [shopping an offer] would create an auction atmosphere!" they said. And they were surely right. However, agents from states where there had been sizzling hot markets—by now at home with bidding wars for property—were not inclined to find this terribly objectionable. "Isn't that a great thing for the seller?" they asked.

Finally, there were those who expressed strong, if not closely reasoned, sentiments that shopping offers was immoral or unethical. These arguments tended to rely on the notion that a buyer's offer is, or should be, confidential.

Ultimately, effective January 1, 2006, an addition was made to Standard of Practice 1-13 that embodied the gist of the 2004 proposal. It holds that, when entering into a buyer or tenant agreement, a Realtor® must advise the client of:

the possibility that sellers or sellers' representatives may not treat the existence, terms, or conditions of offers as confidential unless confidentiality is required by law, regulation, or by any confidentiality agreement between the parties.

Only a few expressed the opinion that, in their states, the terms of a buyer's offer would, under law or regulation, be presumed to be confidential. So, for the most part, if a buyer doesn't want his offer to be shopped, it would be necessary, first, to execute a confidentiality agreement with the seller. While this is theoretically clear, it appears to be practically unlikely to happen.

In terms of the Realtor® Code of Ethics and most, if not all, state laws, Ellen's shopping of the offer was an acceptable thing to do, and surely something she did in an effort to serve her client's interest. Unfortunately for her, and them, it had a very bad result. That, of course, does not make it unethical.

One final note of caution on this topic: If there is a dual-agency situation—suppose the offer had come from another agent in the same company—it is doubtful that it would be ethically acceptable to shop that offer. Why? Because, here, the listing agent (i.e., the broker or firm) is also an agent of the prospective buyer; and shopping the offer would be contrary to that buyer's interest.[23]

---

[23] This point was raised in a 2006 memo from the Legal Department of the California Association of Realtors®.

7

Disclosure

Once upon a time, long ago, in a land far away, disclosure was not a big issue in the practice of real estate. The culture of *caveat emptor* ("buyer beware") ruled the land, and agents, who worked for sellers, were happy. Those days are gone; and they won't come back. In 2001 NAR General Counsel Laurie Janik wrote, "For well over a decade, NAR statistics have shown that the leading sources of litigation against real estate practitioners are lawsuits alleging either misrepresentation or failure to disclose a material fact."[24]

Disclosure litigation expert Bob Brand has estimated that the average cost of a disclosure lawsuit is $25,000 per party (and that includes the 90% of suits that don't go to trial), and the average length of the suit, even though it may finally settle, is one year.[25] The cost of being involved in a suit is not simply financial. It is a drain on the emotions, it can affect one's reputation (regardless of guilt or innocence), and it consumes one's time. During that average one-year period that a suit takes, a participant can expect to devote approximately one-hundred-fifty hours to the proceeding. That's almost one month's work time. It is an amount of time that most people cannot afford to give up.

Whatever the statistics may be, it is fair to say that disclosure issues have become at least one of the central elements to a real estate transaction. For Realtors® this is not confined to disclosure being made about the property. Realtors® also have disclosure obligations

---

[24] In "How Disclosure Forms Reduce Risk," *Realtor® Magazine Online*, January 2001. More recently, in a September 2006 article ("Top Legal Cases: Know Your Risks") in the same publication, NAR Associate Counsel Finley Maxson reports that disclosure issues constitute 13.4% of real estate lawsuits. The major category now is *property management*. However, there may be disclosure-related suits within that category.

[25] Brand's estimates were given in the year 2000. The numbers are likely higher now.

with regard to agency relationships and to their own involvement if they have a personal stake, as principals, in the transaction.

Agent disclosure of property problems is not a natural act. It has to be learned. Problems with the property are potential deal-killers, and agents rightly perceive themselves as deal-makers not deal-killers. (This is true not only of listing agents, but also of buyers' agents. They don't like to see deals get killed either.) But agents can, and do, learn of the need to be diligent about disclosures, and they may even come to see that full disclosure—even if it does result in a dead deal now and then— is really in everybody's interest.

Moreover, for many agents, proper disclosure is likely to be counter-instinctive. Real estate agents are salespeople, after all. It tends to be in both their character and their training that they want to make people happy. Thus, even when making disclosures, they are inclined to elaborate on bare observations in ways that will make people comfort-able. Hence, a crack is a "minor" or "typical" crack. Settling is "nor-mal" and the separation of a walkway from a house is "nothing unusual."

It is just these kinds of characterizations that can get agents in trouble. Bob Brand points out that expert witnesses, with all the appropriate degrees, credentials, and experience, will take the stand and testify that even with all their training, *they* can't tell just by looking that a crack is a *settling* crack, much less that it is a *normal* settling crack. Agents need to learn not to characterize their findings. As Brand says, "Point it out; don't figure it out."

Nor is it always easy to know *what* should be disclosed. Agents have to make judgment calls about which facts are *pertinent*—to use the lan-guage of the Realtor® Code of Ethics—or, as is said more commonly, *material*. Moreover, trying to use Golden Rule thinking here can sometimes mislead us. When we ask ourselves, "Would I want this disclosed to me?" we might legitimately answer, "No, I wouldn't care about that." Yet it might be an issue that is a real concern for the buyer. Sometimes we have to work at putting ourselves in the other person's shoes.

And then there are issues with respect to state and federal laws. There may be some things that would be pertinent to a buyer, yet don't call for disclosure. Let's face it: For some buyers it would be highly relevant to know the racial composition of a neighborhood they are considering. To them, even if *we* think their concerns are misguided, that issue is material. Yet, under fair housing laws, it is not a subject for an agent to report on.

Finally, we acknowledge the problem that can bother the most conscientious of agents, namely, *overdisclosure*. In California, for example, the typical residential transaction generates 18 standard-form disclosures and advisories comprising 37 single-spaced pages. That doesn't include local and company-specific disclosure forms, nor, mind you, the reports generated by whatever inspections are made. One has to wonder if so much disclosure serves a meaningful purpose. The overwhelming volume makes buyers less inclined to read and more inclined just to "sign or initial where indicated." While this is not a problem that is unique to real estate—think medicine, hospitals, and surgical procedures—its commonality does not diminish the negative effects. It is almost as if, in cases like California, a summary page that highlights issues of real importance is needed. But who would want to take on the liability for deciding what not to include? No one who listens to company legal counsel, that's for sure.

Disclosure issues are so involved with the law and liability that it is difficult to think of them in any other context. But disclosure matters are ethical concerns as well. Indeed, the disclosure requirements of the Realtor® Code of Ethics have often run ahead of many state laws. That is, the Code has been known to require *more* in the way of disclosure than some state laws have or do. In fact, if agents will learn and apply the ethical principles involved in disclosure—which may not always be obvious—they will likely stay well within the boundaries of the law.

Material Fact

The other agents had pooh-poohed Armina when she took the vacation rental listing on Lake Drive. It seemed like so much work for so little commission. But, as the years went by, and the same renters returned year after year, it became a lot easier *and* the commissions kept going up.

Now, it had turned into a sale. When the Nobles started renting it out eight years ago, the property was probably worth about $200,000; by now it was in the neighborhood of $750,000, which is what they had listed it for. Let the other agents pooh-pooh her *now*.

Moreover, the sale had gone beautifully. Armina had prepared an exceptional brochure, with not only pictures of the home and the view from its living area but also pictures taken from the lake that showed the boat dock. She even had been able to obtain an aerial photo that demonstrated how the property was oriented to the rest of the lake shore. Of course, she also had the property on plenty of Internet sites, complete with video tours, and in all the slick magazines and nearby newspapers.

She felt good about her advertising efforts, though sometimes she wondered whether it was worth it. The first prospects were brought by a local co-op broker. They were walk-ins—hadn't even seen any of the ads. So what happens? They fell in love with the place at first sight and made a full-price cash offer on the spot. Actually, they offered a fifteen day escrow period, but that had to be extended to thirty, because the owners couldn't get their things out that fast.

It was the second weekend since the home had gone into contract. Lloyd Noble had come up to sort through mementos and furnishings. He had been the family member with whom Armina had had the most contact, so she dropped by just to chat.

Lloyd was in a nostalgic mood. "This sure brings back mixed memories, Armina. There were so many wonderful childhood vacations. But then, after my father took his life here, those just all seemed wiped out. At least it was that way at first. Over time the good memories came back, but even now, on occasion, it is just so painful."

Armina was stunned, on several levels. "Excuse me, Lloyd, but did I understand you correctly? Your father took his life? *Here*? I had never heard anything about that."

"No?" Lloyd responded, " I didn't realize that. But then, I guess I never thought about bringing it up. It had been some years before we decided to rent the place out, so it really didn't occur to me when I met you. Besides, it's kind of personal, and I certainly didn't think it was relevant to our business dealings. Actually, I'm surprised you never heard about it from the Bensons next door. They were living here when it happened."

"No, they never said anything, Lloyd; but actually I have never really talked to them all that much. Just an occasional wave when I drive by. So, no, this is the first I ever heard of it. Do you mind telling me what happened?"

"No, no, I don't mind. It was about eight months after Mom died—it was an auto accident. She died instantly. Dad took her death hard—we really didn't know how bad he was. He hung himself in the garage."

"Oh, Lloyd, I'm so sorry," was about all Armina could muster. They chatted a while longer, and then Armina excused herself to leave.

Back at the office, Armina was so grateful for Hal's calmness. She had always maintained that she couldn't have asked for a better broker.

"Armina, there is certainly no *specific* law that requires that this be disclosed; but you and I both know that the general law and professional ethics obligate the disclosure of material facts, or, as the Code of Ethics puts it, *pertinent* facts. And how do we know if something is a material fact? I've always liked this test: If you don't want to disclose it, then you should.

"Of course, you don't want to disclose this. You're afraid it will kill the deal. I don't blame you. I was kind of looking forward to this closing myself. But we have to do what we have to do. Besides, even though you had never heard anything about this, you can bet that the buyers will learn it from the neighbors after they move in. If it is going to be a problem for them, we don't want to hear about it from their lawyer.

"You had better contact the buyer's agent as soon as you can."

As it turned out, the disclosure didn't kill the deal. One of the buyers' family members had a bit of a problem with it, but she resolved that for herself, and didn't want to block the purchase. Not only that, the buyers expressed their appreciation to Armina for her forthrightness.

Material Fact: Comments and Analysis

It probably won't come as news to anyone reading this book that Realtors® have obligations with respect to disclosing what we might generically call "negative facts" about a property. Actually, the Code (Article 2) states the obligation in a negative way:

> Realtors® shall avoid exaggeration, misrepresenta-
> tion, or *concealment of pertinent facts* relating to the
> property or the transaction. Realtors® shall not,
> however, be obligated to discover latent defects in the
> property, to advise on matters outside the scope of
> their real estate license, or to disclose facts which are
> confidential under the scope of agency or non-agency
> relationships as defined by state law. [*my emphasis*]

State laws and court cases are more likely to put it affirmatively—that there *is* an obligation to disclose, not simply *not to conceal*. Perhaps many will see these as equivalent—that if you have to avoid concealing something, then you have an obligation to make it known or to see to it that it is made known. That is a semantic debate that we shall not try to settle here.

The Code refers to *pertinent* facts. That seems just a little quaint. *Material facts* would probably be the more common expression. And, of course, a variety of definitions are available for *material facts*. In the context of real estate, a material fact may be thought of as anything that might affect the value or desirability of a property, or perhaps anything that would influence one's decision to purchase and/or one's estimate of worth.

While we all may be aware that we have an obligation to disclose known material facts[26], or at least not to conceal them, and even though we have agreed on an appropriate definition, we still may find that, in specific cases, we have disagreements as to whether or not a given fact is material and ought to be disclosed. This is because the term is still inherently subjective. Whether or not a certain fact affects value or desirability ultimately refers to subjective reactions.

In many circumstances, whether or not certain facts are to be deemed *material* has been determined through precedent-setting court decisions and, occasionally, legislation. Under California law, for example, there is no cause of action for failure to disclose the occurrence or manner of any death on a property when that death had occurred more than three years earlier.[27]

However, from an ethical point of view, the law doesn't give us all the answers. Consider the case we just read. Had it taken place in California, neither Armina nor the sellers would have had a *legal* obligation to disclose the occurrence of the suicide. But that doesn't settle the issue from an ethical perspective. Remember, for at least one family member, it did affect the desirability of the property. It would have been, in the words of the Code, a *pertinent fact*. Armina's broker's test was appropriate: "If you don't want to disclose it, you probably should."

Her broker's test is a version of saying, "Would you want it to be disclosed to you?" It is a Golden Rule approach. Looking at situations from the perspective of the Golden Rule may frequently call for behavior that is more sensitive to others than what might be allowed by the law.

---

[26] The qualifier *known* is introduced here. We don't have obligations to disclose things we don't know, though we may be held accountable for not knowing things we *should* have known.

[27] Civil Code Section 1710.2 The statute doesn't say that a death *within* the past three years *must* be disclosed, but it would certainly be advisable to do so.

However, when dealing with highly subjective matters, applying the Golden Rule can be tricky. Suppose a previous occurrence of suicide on the property is something that wouldn't bother you a bit, that would be completely inconsequential to you. Then how do you apply the Golden Rule? If you ask yourself, "Would I want to be told?" your answer might well be "No."

Perhaps the point can be made better with a somewhat less emotionally charged example. Suppose I like pistachio ice cream. Would I be treating my guests with consideration if I gave them pistachio ice cream, as a result of asking myself, "How would I like to be treated?" The Golden Rule needs to be applied at a certain level of generality. I should give my guests what *they* like, because I would want to be given what *I* like. (In my case, that happens to be pistachio, but I can't assume that particular answer for my guests.)

In the real estate context, we don't ask, "Would I want to be told about this particular condition?" Rather, in thinking through the question, "How would I want to be treated?" we see that the answer is, "I would want to be told about anything that someone (agent, principal) thought might possibly affect me."

This still leaves room for errors. That is, there might be a condition that would affect you, and most others might not even consider that possibility.[28] Well, there you have it: Ethics isn't perfect either. You might follow ethical principles to the best of your ability, and something unfortunate still might happen.

In that respect, trying to be ethical is like trying to be good at business. We make the best judgments we can, based on our perception of the facts and the principles that we have learned, but, alas, sometimes things do not turn out as we had hoped.

---

[28] The clearest examples of this happen when we deal with people of different cultures. There may be items of special significance to someone of another cultural heritage, and it might never occur to us that they would be important.

Confidential Information

For Chan it was one of those calls you just love to get. "Hi, Chan, this is Karen. Well, Bob and I are finally ready to do it. Everything has really turned out well in the business—but Bob can tell you about that— and we are ready to move up to a bigger home with a great big view. Of course, we want you to find that home for us," she went on, "but first let's get started by listing ours. Could you come over this evening?"

Could he come over? Could he come over to get started on a listing and a sale? Well, maybe, just this once ... "Karen, I'll be there anytime you say. Does six o'clock work, or would you prefer later?"

Chan had known Bob and Karen for probably ten or twelve years by now. They belonged to the same church; while they weren't close friends—other than church functions, they never socialized together— they still felt a special bond. And, though they had never been engaged in a real estate transaction together—Bob and Karen had bought their present home directly from the builder—they had talked so much about real estate and the purchases and sales made by mutual friends that it felt as if Chan actually had been their agent.

Chan arrived at the appointed hour, and it didn't take long to get from the small talk to the business at hand. It got even better. "Chan, we don't have to sell this house in order to buy what we want. We have the money. We just don't want to keep this one."

After they had walked around the house and talked about things that could be done to prepare it for showing, Bob's voice took on an unusual tone. It was almost as if he thought someone might be listening, and he didn't want them to hear. "Chan, there's something I want to tell you in confidence. It's not a big deal, really; but as our agent I want you to know.

"About two years ago, when we were up at the mountain cabin for a weekend, somehow a pipe came loose in the kids' bathroom. What a mess! I don't know how long the water ran, but by the time we got home there was a pretty good little river running down the stairs, through the family room, under the door to the garage—thank goodness that didn't have a tight threshold—and into the back patio where the drain system picked it up.

"Needless to say, it ruined the stairs and flooring and worked its way into some of the walls too."

"What did you do?" asked a dumbfounded Chan.

"I'll tell you, Chan, if there's a bright side to this story, it is that we found out our insurance company is really good. They sent a claims adjuster out immediately, and the next thing we knew, we had crews in here replacing the floors and stairs, going into the walls, everything. Not only that, after they were through, they sent out a mold inspector or something—I don't know what you call them—and he certified there was no mold or fungus problem. They even sent him back six months later to check again. We got a clean bill of health. I can even show you the certification papers if you want."

"Wow, Bob, that *is* terrific, and I will need a copy of those papers. We'll want to pass them on, along with the story of what happened, to any prospective buyers."

Bob took a deep breath and paused for what felt to Chan like ten minutes. It wasn't, of course. "Chan," he said in a tone that now seemed both confidential and professorial—like he was giving Chan a private lecture—"I told you this was confidential, and I mean for it to stay that way. There is no need to bring all this stuff up to someone who wants to buy the house. You know how skittish people are about mold these days. The mere mention of it turns people away.

"Besides—and this is the important part—we know there is nothing wrong. So, it's not like we're hiding something that could hurt somebody. We're just not going to say anything about it, and that's that."

Now it was Chan's turn to pause. "Bob, I want to list Karen's and your house. I want to because we are friends, and because it is a great business opportunity that you are giving me—one that I really appreciate. But I just don't know about this. Please, let me talk to my broker in the morning, and then I will get back to you."

The next day Chan called with his broker's opinion, one that had not surprised him. His broker said that absolutely they would have to disclose this, and they could not list the property otherwise.

Bob wasn't surprised. "Actually, Chan, after you left, Karen and I discussed this at some length. It's nothing personal, and it certainly shouldn't affect our friendship. But it's clear that on some things we just may not see eye to eye. I think, and Karen does too, that we'll all be better off—and remain better friends—if we just don't get tangled up in any real estate deals together. They say it's not a good idea to work with friends anyway. We are going to list with that guy who is always sending us mailers and walking around the neighborhood. He seems a decent fellow, and he's already told Karen he would love to find a new house for us when we are ready to move."

A few months later, Chan saw on the MLS hot sheet that Bob and Karen's house had been listed. He knew that they had already purchased their new house through Jeff—that guy who sent them mailers and walked their neighborhood—so he was not surprised to see that Jeff had the listing.

Actually, Chan and Jeff had always been on good terms and had mutual respect for each other's professional abilities. So no hostility was presumed, or intended, when Chan called and congratulated Jeff on listing Bob and Karen's house. He just had one question: "How are you going to handle the disclosure about the interior flooding and mold remediation?"

"I don't know what the hell you are talking about," Jeff replied.

"Well, let me tell you what I know," Chan began.

Confidential Information: Comments and Analysis

Almost every residence has a flaw, circumstance, or history that might be a problem for some buyer. And there are plenty of sellers who wouldn't want that to be brought up. If you have had a good number of listings, you've probably experienced some version of this. If you have a career ahead of you, you probably will.

Sometimes these issues are not revealed by the seller. They may be uncovered by a third-party inspection. The seller might not even have had previous knowledge of the situation. Nonetheless, there are sellers who don't want the information to go any further. This is what happened in Case Interpretation 1-25.[29]

The situation here raises two basic questions for agents: (1) What do I do if a seller refuses to disclose a defect and instructs me not to as well? (2) What are we limited from doing if the seller says that this information is confidential?

The answer to the first question is contained in the answer given by Chan's broker. Essentially, it is, "Run away. Run far, far away." Seriously, you just don't want to be a part of anything like this. There is an old saw that "no deal is worth your reputation." By the same token, no deal is worth your license. And that's the sort of thing you are talking about here. Not to mention the lawsuit.

The somewhat tricky part is that this kind of issue can arise at different times within a listing history. In our story, it was at the pre-listing stage, so there was just (*just!*) the matter of not taking the listing. But a similar situation could arise during the course of a listing or even when a property is under contract. In either of those situations, if the seller wants you to violate both your ethical and legal obligations, you really have only one choice. Bail out. Resign from the relationship.

In both of those cases you might still have a claim on commission or some compensation. That would be a matter to discuss with your company attorney.

---

[29] In the spirit of full disclosure, I acknowledge that this Case Interpretation trades on themes that are quite similar to the scenario in *Confidential Information*. But I do not confess to plagiarism. Regrettably, *Confidential Information* is one of those scenarios that came out of our own personal experience. It was written before I ever saw Case Interpretation 1-25.

What about the confidential information part? Fortunately, the Realtor® Code of Ethics is very clear on this point. Standard of Practice 1-9 says:

> Information concerning latent material defects is not considered confidential information under this Code of Ethics.

Not only do you have a right to share such information with future agents and/or principals, it could be argued that you have an ethical obligation to do so. This is not something you will find spelled out in the Realtor® Code of Ethics, but it is certainly something the Golden Rule might have you do. Suppose you were buying the house. Would you want someone to tell you?

Suppose you were the new listing agent. Would you want to know about the problem? You should. In real estate, ignorance is not bliss.

Agent Interest

Victor was a successful Realtor® who felt like he was getting nowhere. There was no question about the success: Rookie of the Year in his first year, Double Diamond level production the next two, and then Triple Diamond—the franchise's highest level—the year after that. Yet not a lot to show for it.

Sure, he and Chris had been able to buy a really nice house—and the mortgage payments gave him even more motivation—and they had shiny new cars. They took some really nice vacations and even joined the tennis club. But they were a big zero when it came to investments— no income property, no stock holdings, *nada*. He was making lots of money, but he wasn't creating wealth.

It was Chris' dad, Dale, who, in a very kind and gentle father-in-law way, came to the rescue. That had been not quite two years ago.

"Vic, I have a proposal for you. I think it will be good for me, and I think it will be good for you and Chris—it's one of those win-win deals."

Chris' dad was the lead man in a small but solid LLC that had been buying and managing investment properties throughout the county for the past eight years. It had always seemed unduly brash for Victor to attempt to solicit their business, and he and Dale had never broached the subject. Today was different."

"Vic, the agent who has worked with our little investment group is going to be moving out of the area. Well, you know I admire the way you work and the success you have had. I'd like to give you the opportunity to handle our business.

"Wow," Victor began, but Dale cut him off.

"However, I want to put a little twist on this. I've talked it over with the others, and they all agree. Here's what we propose:

"Every time you represent us in a purchase—we're not going to be selling anything for a long time—when escrow closes you will rebate half of your commission directly into our LLC account. But we're not asking you to work for half the going rate; we're going to help you get started on an investment program. You see, once your commission rebates have totaled up to $50,000, then you will be vested at a 5% interest in the LLC, no strings attached, no further rebates required.

"I know 5% doesn't sound like a very big stake, but I think you'll find that it will become 5% of a pretty substantial portfolio."

No one could have been a more diligent buyer's agent than Victor became for the LLC. Truth be told, he put in way more time locating properties and structuring transactions than even full commissions would have merited; but with every closing—*cha ching!*—he got one step closer to that investment interest. He loved it, Chris loved it, and, of course, Dale was pleased as punch.

If Victor could put *this* deal together, it would put him over the top of the $50,000 mark. But he was going to have to work for it.

Practically every real estate agent in town had heard of old man Blanchard. The Blanchard family had been among the first settlers in the county, and there were plenty of Blanchard-owned properties around to show for it. Sam Blanchard controlled most of the family properties, and he had slowly been selling them off. All "For Sale by Owner."

So it was no surprise to Victor when Sam quoted to him his number one rule of selling real estate, "Never use an agent." "I don't have anything against you boys," Sam told him; "I just never could see why I should pay someone so much just to put up a sign and wait for someone else to bring me a buyer. I never minded paying a commission to a buyer's agent, though; I figure you guys do the work."

Although Victor had done nothing to encourage it, Sam went on. "I've got another rule too. I never sell to a real estate guy. I figure, if I do, I'm probably not getting enough. I know you people—you don't buy unless it's a deal, do you? Well, I don't want anyone to be getting a deal from me.

"So, by the way, you seem awfully interested in this property for an agent. You're not one of the buyers, are you?"

"No, sir," Victor replied. "Along with the purchase proposal, I've given you a profile of the group—it's called an LLC—which includes something about all of the members. You'll probably recognize most of the names. They're people who have been around here for some time, and they're all solid citizens. As you'll see, my name isn't among them."

Victor had taken care of it all. Most of the due diligence work was done before they even made the offer. Sam was happy to sign a nonagency agreement but still pay a handsome commission. Everything went as it should, and the closing was right on time. Finally, Victor and Chris were going to start building wealth.

Agent Interest: Comments and Analysis

Article 4 of the Realtor® Code of Ethics reads as follows:

> Realtors® shall not acquire an interest in or buy or present
> offers from themselves, any member of their immediate
> families, their firms or any member thereof, or any entities
> in which they have any ownership interest, any real prop-
> erty without making their true position known to the
> owner or the owner's agent or broker. In selling property
> they own, or in which they have any interest, Realtors®
> shall reveal their ownership or interest in writing to the
> purchaser or the purchaser's representative.

What is the basis of this ethics requirement? Would you want to know,
if you were on the other side? You might not care if it were a real estate
agent, or if the agent had some interest in the transactions. But how
about others? This is another one of those twists on applying the
Golden Rule. *You* might not care about having an agent on the other
side of a transaction with you. But if you were in the shoes of a
nonagent , don't you think you might want to know?

Why would someone want to know if the purchaser were a real estate
licensee? There is a presumption here that a real estate person might
know things that the seller doesn't know. Actually, that was reflected
in Sam Blanchard's explanation of his (second) rule. He didn't want to
sell to real estate agents because he figured that they would have seen a
deal, that they saw something that he didn't.[30]

The disclosure requirement puts the seller on notice. It doesn't
necessarily take away the knowledge advantage that a Realtor® might
possibly have. Suppose you, a Realtor®, happen to have some information, or strong belief, about future development that makes a particu-

---

[30] Obviously, just refusing to sell to a real estate agent wouldn't have advanced
Sam's position. The presumption is that an agent's interest would lead him to
start researching his property more closely and to adjust the price accordingly.

lar property seem attractive. You don't have to give the information to the owner or seller; you just have to let them know who you are.[31]

Let us turn to the specifics of our case. Did Victor violate the Realtor® Code of Ethics? He might have argued that he didn't, on the following grounds: (1) At the time, he had no ownership interest in the LLC. (2) He was not bringing the offer on behalf of his father-in-law: he was representing the LLC. (3) Anyway, his father-in-law is not an immediate family member, which is what the Code mentions.

His defense would not wash. Defense (1) is just "lawyering." It is not in the spirit of the Code, which, if you look at the Case Interpretations for Article 4, is very important. Nor are defenses (2) and (3). It is very instructive to look at Case Interpretations 4-2 and 4-3. The former makes it clear that not every indirect relationship, no matter how "stretched," is going to require disclosure. In this respect, the Code seems somewhat more lenient or realistic (you choose) than rulings that sometimes come down about conflicts of interest in government affairs or as understood by legal firms. On the other hand, the latter, Case Interpretation 4-3, also shows that the "spirit" of the Code is probably more important than literal interpretation.

We note that the Code is symmetrical with respect to these issues. A Realtor®'s interest status in a transaction needs to be disclosed whether the Realtor® is on the buying or the selling end. The law, as we have noted in Chapter 1 (page 10), is not necessarily so. California, for example, requires disclosure of a licensee's status to a buyer, but not necessarily to a seller.

While the Code may be symmetrical in this regard, the reasoning is somewhat different. A seller is put on notice about a Realtor®'s interest in a property, because the Realtor® might know something about the property, or its potential, that the seller doesn't know. Presumably, what the Realtor® might know would be a good thing about the property. That would be why the Realtor® wants to acquire it.

---

[31] Both the Code (Standard of Practice 4-1) and good sense require that you document this in writing.

On the other hand, the disclosure of a Realtor®'s ownership interest to a buyer is not based on the fact that the Realtor® might know some bad thing about the property that the buyer doesn't know. There are already other Code and legal requirements that take care of that. If there is some negative feature that the Realtor® knows, he already has to tell the buyer.

So what is the reason that a Realtor®'s status as a seller would have to be disclosed? The assumption here is that the buyer should be put on notice, because the Realtor® may be better at bargaining than the buyer. Sometimes, that is true.

8

Relations with Affiliates

There is no precise definition of what constitutes an *affiliate*. Some Realtor® associations allow almost any business that desires to become an affiliate member to do so. Others seek to draw the line at "those who provide real estate-related services," but that net can be cast pretty wide too, so that you have members who are carpet cleaners, gardeners, etc. For the purposes of this chapter, the term *affiliates* is generally meant to denote those who are sometimes described as "settlement service providers." Think of those whose payment is likely to show up on a closing statement—escrow, title, and mortgage companies; home inspectors; pest control operators; home warranty providers; closing attorneys; etc.[32]

Not only are affiliates an integral part of our business life, but in many settings they are also vital to the functioning of the local board or association. Associations may be dependent on affiliates for their labor and/or their financial support. In fact, some real estate firms and agents may be similarly dependent.

Whether a Realtor® is dependent on an affiliate or affiliates or whether he or she is just the recipient of a variety of benefits, the situation can become a bit dicey. First of all, there may be legal issues. These may involve RESPA and/or state laws. Now, in this text we are not going to arrive at a final, clear-cut, easy-to-apply set of criteria as to what is and what is not a RESPA violation.[33] But you don't have to be a RESPA wizard to grasp the main point: Namely, they—that is,

---

[32] Of course, there can be persons who receive payment through a closing— e.g., painters or contractors—who would not be considered "settlement service providers."

[33] Probably no one is going to come up with such a definition or set of criteria. Nonetheless, these are topics that bear much discussion in office meetings and at association levels.

settlement service providers such as lenders, title and escrow companies, home warranty firms, and home inspectors—aren't supposed to
give us stuff for the referral of business or as an inducement to refer
business. Moreover, we—real estate licensees—are not supposed to
accept stuff from them under those conditions. [What I have called
"stuff" is rendered as "things of value" in RESPA parlance.] It is
sometimes difficult to grasp this notion, simply because (practically)
"everyone does it."

To this, someone might say, "So, what's the harm? After all, as you
said, just about everybody does it. And we've all been doing it for
years. Yet things seem to be working all right. We're not talking about
gigantic consumer rip-offs. This is mostly petty stuff; and, frankly, it
helps to make the system work a whole lot better. Lighten up already."

I understand that point of view. I once held it. But I have come to
believe that it is seriously mistaken, for there is harm, real harm.

One sort of harm that results from some of the persistent RESPA
violations that occur at an agent level is that the occasional straight
shooter, or even just the naïf who doesn't get the benefits, is put at a
competitive disadvantage. I doubt that there are many market areas in
the country where there is not at least one (probably more than one)
high-producing agent who has a significant amount of his or her
advertising costs picked up by a title or mortgage company. (I mean
paid either in whole or in a disproportionate part by them—not in
compliance with HUD's requirements.) Of course, this enables that
agent to advertise in greater volume and more elaborately than the
unsubsidized agent. It makes it more difficult for the latter to compete.

The harm brought about by persistent RESPA violations is not confined to the creation of uneven playing fields for agents and their
firms. There is a more subtle and damaging harm that affects the
industry as a whole. It is simply that the ethical climate in which we
would like to operate is undermined by a widespread and, frankly,
cynical disregard for the law.

If a parent habitually ignores traffic laws and openly talks about
evading jury duty and scamming the tax system, his children are not

going to pay a lot of attention to noble lectures about law and order. Likewise, if an agent sees that his broker is on the take—that the firm accepts (frequently, *seeks*) illegal subsidies, favors, and gratuities—or that his broker tolerates such activity by other agents in the firm, then that agent is not going to be terribly impressed by company pronouncements about the importance of professional ethics and principled behavior. The same goes for associations.

Even if there were no such laws as RESPA or the corresponding state regulations, Realtors® still would need to be sensitive to the conflicts of interest that may arise when they have become used to accepting gifts and support from various affiliates. Too often I have heard the choice of a particular service provider justified on the grounds that "they give terrific service," when the service alluded to was, in fact, for the benefit of the Realtor®, not the principals.

Finally, in thinking about our relationships with affiliates, we need to address a topic that isn't dealt with by the Realtor® Code of Ethics but that is all too common. Realtors® need to be sensitive to an all-too-easy propensity to abuse affiliates in the way they are treated. This may extend from simple issues of manners to serious questions of ethics. We need to be careful not to treat affiliates in a manner that just takes them for granted or that demands special treatment. Worse yet, more than one broker or agent has made demands of an affiliate that put that person on the spot, sometimes pushing them over the edge of legal lines. Realtors® shouldn't do that. We should treat affiliates with the kind of respect that we would like to be shown. It's a Golden Rule thing.

Debt of Gratitude

Susan didn't really care that much for baseball games, but she had to admit this big-league stadium was really something. It made her wonder if this was what the Roman circus was like. In any event, the trip, sponsored by Silverland Title, was a lot of fun (the bus trip was a total hoot), and it was good to get away for a day and see so many agent-friends in a relaxed setting. Besides, she really did need to do a little "prenegotiating" with Lupe about that Country Club Drive listing, and this Clubhouse restaurant was a perfect place to chat.

"I don't care that much about baseball either," Lupe began, "but if we can sit here in air-conditioned comfort, enjoy lunch and some nice wine at Jerry's expense, while we watch those hunks run around in their silly uniforms—well, I guess that's as good a setting to talk about business as anywhere. So, tell me, Susie Q., what do we have going? Are you going to bring me an offer?"

"I think so, my dear. You saw how they were all gaga at the open house. Their main hang-up right now is about how to access the rear yard, so that he can have a place to keep his toys—the boat and the ATV carrier. I suppose they could redo that side yard and go in from there; but that's going to cost a fair amount of money, and you've got to admit, your folks are already asking top dollar."

"Well, yes, that is what they are *asking* ...," Lupe began, but she was interrupted by Jerry's arrival at the table.

"Good afternoon, ladies. You know you're not going to catch any foul balls in here," he began with a little chuckle, "but that's OK. We just want to be sure you have a good time. I'm so glad you could come; your business has meant a lot to me."

"Well, we sure appreciate all that you and Silverland do for us, Jerry," responded Susan. "Speaking of which, I hope you haven't filled up that continuing ed seminar and luncheon next week. I really want to go—I love that hotel's restaurant—and I just haven't gotten around to signing up yet."

"Susie, we've always got a spot for you. I'll take care of getting you signed up. All you have to do is show up. Anyway, I don't want to interrupt you two any further. Just a 'by the way' for you, Lupe. Your 'Just Listed' postcards are going out this afternoon. I saw them at our printers last night. They look terrific. Enjoy the game, you two, or the lunch, or the wine. Whatever ..." And Jerry was off on his way to another table.

"He's such a good guy," Susan commented as Jerry made his way around the room. "I'll tell you, that contact management software he set up for me—with the flyer templates, and those keep-in-touch letters and postcards, and all the other stuff—it just changed my real estate life. To think that I used to print out labels myself and lug all that stuff down to the post office. Now, I just select what I want, email the order to Silverland, and poof—it's done!"

Lupe nodded in agreement. "He *has* been terrific."

It wasn't long before they got the Country Club Drive deal together. Lupe's folks came down, as she had thought they would, so that Susan's buyers were comfortable with the prospect of having to spend something later to get that access right. As was typical, neither buyer nor seller had a favorite title company (frankly, neither one of them really knew what a title company did); they left those details to the agents. As the seller told Lupe, "That's one reason we hire an agent. You know about these things; we don't."

"I presume you want to go with Jerry," Susan semi-queried.

"Oh, yeah," Lupe responded. "You know, I've heard that Silverland is one of the most expensive around, but I figure you get what you pay for. I mean, look at the service they give." Susan nodded in agreement.

"In fact," Lupe went on, "this deal looks so good, I think I'll call Jerry and order my 'Just Sold' cards now. I'll bet he can have them in the mail the day we close!"

Debt of Gratitude: Comments and Analysis

So what, if anything, is wrong here? What has just been described is as common as can be. Well, maybe not everyone gets treated to Clubhouse Level lunch at a big-league ball park, but it's a sure thing that every day, somewhere, some settlement service provider is chosen, not by a principal, but by a Realtor® who is in some way indebted to the provider or one of its reps.

Some may be thinking that there are RESPA violations going on, and that's a relevant consideration; but it's not something to be explored here. Sometimes it is absolutely clear that a given activity is a RESPA violation, and some instances are discussed elsewhere in this text. But, frequently, when there is talk of RESPA violations, it becomes an occasion for lawyering, qualifying, and looking for loopholes. Realtors® can be very skilled and creative about this. So can many of their affiliate counterparts. So we are not going to get into that in this section.

Here, we want to approach these matters more generally. Without raising questions about the law, let us just consider the issue of making recommendations when we have a conflict of interest.

Consider this similarity between real estate agents and doctors: In both cases, practitioners are showered with gifts—ranging from small monetary value to substantial—from those whose business it is to sell products and services to their clients or patients. In the medical arena the gift-givers are pharmaceutical companies and the makers of medical devices. In the world of real estate they are title companies, mortgage companies, escrow firms, termite companies, home inspectors, and others. In all cases, the givers of gifts are hoping that the practitioner will direct or advise a third party (client, patient) to purchase their product or service.

This clearly creates a potential conflict of interest. Is the doctor, or the real estate agent, recommending the product or service on the basis of quality and/or price, or does the recommendation come as a result of the gift-giving?

There is no body of law that prohibits pharmaceutical and other medical companies from using gifts, subsidies, entertainment, and other enticements to try to influence physicians to recommend and prescribe their products. Policies in that regard must come from the codes of ethics adopted by the various medical association governing bodies.

The medical profession has taken these conflict-of-interest issues quite seriously. As a result of increasing concern, during the 1980s the

American Medical Association conducted a study of the issues that resulted in adoption of a set of ethical guidelines relative to gift-giving practices. Subsequent studies have resulted in even more stringent recommendations.

In September 2006 Stanford University Medical Hospital and Clinics joined Yale and the University of Pennsylvania in adopting a zero-tolerance policy regarding gifts from pharmaceutical and other industry representatives. They won't even allow the acceptance of pens or notepads.

What about the real estate community? Here, the customs and practice of gift-giving are every bit as much a way of life as they have been in the medical profession. Only more so. For some agents and firms, the largesse bestowed by affiliated service providers is not just a nice benefit; it is a vital contributor to the bottom line—one that is consciously counted on.

Yet, as a profession, we have not shown the same degree of concern about such practices as medicine has shown. But the problem, of course, is the same. How can real estate agents fulfill their fiduciary duties to their clients if their advice and/or choices may be influenced by the relationship created through various gifts and subsidies?[34]

The traditional response to a conflict-of-interest problem has been to advocate disclosure. Thus Article 6 of the Realtor® Code of Ethics says:

> When recommending real estate products or services (e.g., homeowner's insurance, warranty programs, mortgage financing, title insurance, etc.), Realtors® shall disclose to the client or customer to whom the recommendation is made any financial benefit or fees,

---

[34] Realtors® need to be particularly careful as to how they may attempt to justify their recommendations. Sometimes they will say, as in the story, that the company or rep in question gives "great service," but often that refers to service that benefits the Realtor®, not necessarily the client.

other than real estate referral fees, the Realtor® or
Realtor® firm may receive as a direct result of such
recommendation.

This admonition is laudable so far as it goes, but it is woefully incom-
plete with respect to the problem. In particular, it is to be noted that
the disclosure requirement applies only to the Realtor®'s receipt of
future benefits, as if there were a specific tit-for-tat arrangement in play.
But there is no disclosure requirement regarding already-received
benefits that well may have served as an inducement to give the referral
in the first place.[35]

Secondly, and more telling, is the more general finding that conflict-of-
interest disclosures have little effect anyway. George Lowenstein, an
economics professor at Carnegie Mellon who has done research on
this topic, puts it this way: "If you disclose a conflict of interest, people
in general don't know how to use that information. And, to the extent
that they do anything at all, they actually tend to underestimate the
severity of these conflicts."

Having a conflict of interest is not in and of itself an ethical failing.
Conflicts may be created as a result of a variety of different circumstances, some of them beyond our control. The ethical question arises
with respect to how we handle the conflict. We must be sure to put
our client's interest above, not only our prospective future benefit, but
also above our feelings of indebtedness or gratitude.

---

[35] The powerful influence of past behavior is overlooked too easily and too
often. Social science research has shown that even the giving of small gifts or
benefits may create a significant feeling of indebtedness or gratitude. Doctors,
when surveyed, said that they did not believe that they were influenced by the
various small gifts and benefits they received. But a majority of them also said
that they believed that most of their colleagues *were* influenced by such
things!

Lender's Helper

"I tell you, Sandy, I am really getting discouraged." Art kind of aimlessly toyed with his chopsticks. "I just feel like I'm getting squeezed from every direction. Expenses are up all over the place. My website costs more, all the supplies have gone up, my assistant wants a raise, the transaction coordinator is charging more—for crying out loud, it even costs more to have lunch here! But, if anything, my income is shrinking. Oh, I'm holding my own in volume, even with the downturn; but I just make less on every transaction. I can't believe the squeeze on commissions with all the competition—of course, you know about that—and then it seems like I wind up chipping in to fix torn screens, or who knows what, just to get the deal to close. I never minded doing that before, but now it's beginning to hurt."

"Well, Art, you're not going to change the prices of things, so you need to look at increasing your income ..."

"Oh, thanks," Art interrupted, only half-jokingly, "I never thought of that. I'll just go out and make some more sales, and then everything will be OK. Why didn't that occur to me?"

"Oh, stop it, Art; you know I'm not riding you like that. I'm serious, my friend," Sandy went on, her voice somewhat hushed now. "I've come across a way to make more money on just about every deal where I represent the buyer. As a matter of fact, that's why I asked you to have lunch today. I wanted to tell you about it. Of course, the fact that I'll get a nice little referral fee if you're interested had something to do with it too." She laughed lightly, and Art's mood seemed to ease up a bit.

"My dear, you have my undivided attention. Tell me all about it."

"Well, you know Matt Benson, the mortgage rep ..." Art nodded. "He came to me at the beginning of the year with a proposal. He said that if I could work with his company—not as a loan rep or anything like that—I could make some serious extra money on transactions where I had some kind of control over the buyer's loan choices."

"Oh, Sandy, don't tell me you've crossed over the RESPA lines and you're taking referrals for loan business. You know not to do that, and you know I'm not going to ..."

Sandy shushed him. "No, no, it's not that at all. This is perfectly straight up. I don't get referrals; I earn the money." Art looked dubious. "I mean, it's not a *lot* of work, but it is a bit of a drag, and it takes some time. What I do is to take the buyer's loan application, and you know that's not just a little walk in the park. I have to explain the 1003, which isn't exactly the world's friendliest form, and then I tell them what they need to look up or find out and how to put things in the best light. You know: all that stuff. I pretty much walk them through it. It's a lot more than a referral.

"But the pay adds up. I get half a point on each loan; so you're talking a thousand to two thousand dollars per transaction in this marketplace. I'll tell you, Art, it's made a big difference. You should look into it."

Art didn't need a lot of prodding. He was on the phone to Matt the next morning, and Matt was in his office that afternoon.

"Are you a broker, Art?" Matt asked after they had gone over most of the details, which were just as Sandy had described.

"No, just an honest salesperson," Art replied.

"Oh, that's OK, I just don't know if Sandy told you about the payment part. I'm sure you understand that we can't pay you directly; we want to do everything on the up-and-up. So we'll have to make payment to your broker. We do this with lots of our agents. The brokers never have a problem, though usually they want their normal split."

It wasn't a problem for Tina, Art's broker, either. In fact she liked the idea so much, she thought all her agents should be doing it—and she should be getting her usual split.

Matt was scheduled to address the office meeting next Tuesday morning. He even offered to bring the doughnuts.

Lender's Helper: Comments and Analysis

It has already been noted that this is not a text of legal dos and don'ts. There is so much vagueness and unclarity in the law that any prudent person must hesitate before pronouncing that *this* behavior is legally OK, but *that* behavior is not. Moreover, no matter how confident even the most educated and experienced person might feel about such a judgment, one can probably find an equally credentialed person who would argue the other side.

Still, some matters *are* clear—or, at least, there is consensus about them—and they do need to be pointed out. That is true of a large part of fair housing law, and it is true of at least some parts of RESPA interpretation. This is one of those parts.

The proposition offered by Matt, the mortgage rep, certainly has its appeal (even though it may be modest by the standards of some market areas), but it also has an air of legitimacy. It wasn't just a naked payment-for-referral arrangement. The agent did have to do some work for the payment, and, by insisting that payment be made to or through a broker, there was an up-and-up air about it. It's just that, as we shall see, in the eyes of HUD, there wasn't *enough* work involved.

But let me be clear: I don't necessarily want to condemn Matt or his real-world counterparts for making the offer, for he well may not have known that it was a violation. (To be sure, in a strict sense, he *should* have known, and could be held accountable.) I couldn't begin to count how many affiliates from a variety of businesses (escrow, title, lending, home warranty, etc.) I have known who, in all innocence, have pro-posed programs and engaged in activities that were, in fact, in viola-tion of federal and/or state law. In most cases, they had been told that the activity in question was perfectly OK by experienced colleagues, their managers, real estate brokers, or others who they thought would be reliable sources of information.

We learn so much in this business through examples and word of mouth. Alas, it's not always correct.

In 2004 the Legal Affairs Department of the National Association of Realtors® issued a white paper titled *HUD's Guidelines: When a Mortgage Company May Pay a Fee to a Third Party for Loan Origination Work without Violating RESPA.* The central point of the paper is this: *"HUD has made clear that the mere taking of a loan application is not sufficient work to justify a fee under RESPA."* [my emphasis] The paper goes on to say:

> HUD generally would be satisfied that no §8 RESPA violation had occurred if a real estate salesperson (1) took information from the borrower and filled out the loan application; (2) performed at least five additional items on the Loan Origination Services List (attached hereto); and (3) received a fee reasonably related to the market value of the services performed.

The list of Loan Origination Services, at least five of which are to be performed in addition to taking the loan application, follows:

Loan Origination Services List

According to HUD, some or all of the following services are normally performed in the origination of a loan:

(a) taking information from borrower and filling out application;

(b) analyzing borrower's income and debt and pre-qualifying him to determine maximum mortgage he can afford;

(c) educating borrower in home buying and financing process, advising him about different types of loan products available, demonstrating how closing costs and monthly payments would vary under each product;

(d) collecting financial information (tax returns, bank statements) and other related documents that are part of application process;

(e) initiating/ordering verifications of employment and verifications of deposits;

(f) initiating/ordering requests for mortgage and other loan verifications;

(g) initiating/ordering appraisals;

(h) initiating/ordering inspections or engineering reports;

(i) providing disclosures (truth in lending, good faith estimate, others) to borrower;

(j) assisting borrower in understanding clearing credit problems;

(k) maintaining regular contact with borrower, realtors and lender between application and closing to apprise them of status of application and to gather additional information needed;

(l) ordering legal documents;

(m) determining whether property is located in flood zone (or ordering such service); and

(n) participating in the loan closing.

Source: HUD Informal Op. No. 13.

We've all heard the expression, "If something sounds too good to be true, it probably isn't." There is a RESPA corollary: "If a money-making program sounds too easy to be legal, it probably isn't."

Difficult Appraisal

"Terry, this is Chet, the appraiser." It was the fifth message on Terry's answer phone. "I have to tell you that I'm having trouble with the job for that Blue Mountain property. I mean, there just aren't a lot of comps for a 10-bedroom house with a private landing strip and a two-acre pond stocked with bass.

"I don't see how I'm going to be able to bring it in at the $6.5 million purchase price. We have that one other on Old Smokey that had seven bedrooms, tennis courts, and the stables. But, still, that was only $4.75 mil. There are a couple of parcels that had land values of three million, but their value was in the lot split potential.

"Bottom line: I just don't see how I'm going to make it. We just don't have the matches."

Actually, Terry was glad that he didn't have to speak with Chet. He probably would have said something he would later regret. Better to leave a message. "Listen, Chet, I appreciate that this isn't easy. But, hey, that's why you get the big bucks, right? Anyway, I can tell you that you're going to have to go over to Iron Lakes to pick up some more comps for this sale.

"I don't care if it's a town five miles away. You're not going to find something within ten blocks of the Blue Mountain property. This isn't a tract house you're appraising; it's not a plan B.

"Anyway, the big homes in Iron Lakes are the ones that compete with our estate properties here. When people fly out here to buy a fancy-dancy vacation mansion, they look here and they look there. We're both the same distance from the airport. They don't care whether it's here or in Iron Lakes. They just want something that will knock their guests' socks off.

"Besides, you know this isn't a loan appraisal that's going to be reviewed somewhere. It's a cash deal. The buyer isn't going to care that you use Iron Lakes comps; he's looked there too. Like I said. Anyway, he just wants the appraisal so he doesn't feel like he's done something stupid."

After Terry hung up, he just buried his head in his hands. "It's hard enough making the sale," he thought. "Do I have to do everyone *else's* work too?"

It was another answer machine message, which was fine with Terry. "Terry, it's Chet again. Hey, thanks for that suggestion about looking at Iron Lakes. That was a great idea, and I was able to pull some more comparable properties.

"That was the good news. Problem is ... I still can't get the value up there. Even with the Iron Lakes comps, it still comes in at $5.75 million. I'm sorry; but that's what it is. I'm about to print it up, so if you have any further thoughts, please give me a call."

Terry was glad to reach Chet directly this time. As a matter of fact, he declined to leave messages the last two times he tried. This wasn't something he particularly wanted on tape.

"Chet, you do a lot of appraisals for Community Action Bank, don't you?"

"I sure do, Terry. They're probably 40% of my business."

"Well, Chet, you may know that the broker of my office, Dennis Arends, is also a director of that bank ..."

"No, I didn't."

"Well, he is, Chet, and he had a talk with the bank president a few hours ago. Feel free to call him and confirm this if you'd like. Anyway, they both agreed that you probably need to sharpen up your pencil and rework the numbers on that Blue Mountain appraisal. Heck, we know that 90% of those adjustment figures are picked out of the air anyway."

"So, you do that Chet; and get back to me when you have it at purchase value. That Community Action account has got to be a good one. It would be a shame to lose it."

Difficult Appraisal: Comments and Analysis

For some years now it has been a bit of a slogan that the Realtor® is, or should be, "at the center of the transaction." Generally, it is true, and as a result, it puts the Realtor® in a position of considerable influence. Not only does the Realtor® exercise influence in the recommendation—sometimes the outright choice—of various service providers, but also he or she is liable to have considerable interaction with those persons. This can be a very good thing and a tremendous benefit for the client. It also carries with it a serious potential for abuse.

The not-so-subtle threat that Terry, along with his broker and the bank president, brought against Chet, the appraiser, might well constitute a crime in many states. (Federal law probably wouldn't be an issue here, because there was no loan involved.) In any case, his doing so was surely ethically wrong. A simple application of the Golden Rule would tell us this. Certainly, we wouldn't want to be treated that way if we were in the other person's shoes. Moreover, what Terry was trying to do can also be seen as a violation of Article 1 of the Realtor® Code of

Ethics. Article 1 obligates a Realtor® to treat all parties to the transaction honestly. Any attempt on the part of a listing agent to falsify a report or to misstate a finding is going to be a violation of that obligation.

Appraisers, home inspectors, and structural pest control inspectors are all potential targets for pressure to alter their findings. Realtors® should be very sensitive to their ethical obligation to avoid pressuring them.

Now, I am certainly not saying that Realtors® ought not to involve themselves with inspectors and that they should never challenge someone's findings. There are many judgment calls in the various reports that are prepared during a purchase transaction, and many times they may be open to dispute.

If a Realtor® thinks an appraisal is too low, or too high for that matter, he certainly has the right, probably even an obligation to his client, to challenge that result. (A lot of appraisers won't like this.) What Terry did at the outset is perfectly appropriate. He was trying to steer the appraiser in the right direction. More than a few times I have known appraisers to appreciate Realtors® supplying different comps or, even more to the point, a different perspective, that resulted in a more appropriate valuation. It can be a collaborative effort. It need not be contentious.

The situation is similar with respect to other inspectors as well. Home inspections may involve a variety of judgment calls, and some of them may be incorrect. (This is certainly not meant as a general criticism of home inspectors.) They may even be mistaken about whether or not a certain item conforms to building code requirements. If a Realtor® has a disagreement with an inspector, he should pursue that. But he should pursue it with facts and reasons, not threats.

Nor, for that matter, should a Realtor® employ a carrot rather than the stick. It is just as objectionable, and frequently illegal, to attempt to influence the outcome of a report (appraisal, pest control, home inspection, whatever) by offering some benefit—financial or otherwise—to the person who is preparing it.

9

Relations with Other Agents

Anyone who has been in the real estate business for a while can tell you at least two things about relationships with other agents. One is that some of the best friendships they have ever had have been formed with other Realtors®. This is especially true of those who involve themselves in the activities of the local, state, and national associations. Another thing they can tell you is that some of their competitors are people they can't stand, don't trust, and hope to never be involved with in a transaction.

So there you have it: The types of people you'll find involved in the real estate business pretty well cover the spectrum of the types of people you find in the world.

Realtors® are competitors who are committed to cooperate with each other and to respect each other's relationships with their clients. The latter is not always easy to do. Partly, that is because to do so is not exactly instinctive; and partly it is because the rules for doing so are more than a little complex. Some of the most contentious disputes among Realtors® occur over charges of encroaching on, or failing to respect, one's agency relationship with a principal. There are times when such charges may be justified, but there are other times when they may be based on a misunderstanding of the Realtor® Code of Ethics.

It is understandable that Realtors® may feel unclear and sometimes even confused on the Code of Ethics rules that apply with respect to not taking actions that are "inconsistent with exclusive representation or exclusive brokerage relationship agreements." This is an area that provides a good example of the need for professional codes. When we deal with agency relationships that arise out of exclusive-representation agreements, we are far, far away from the situations of our everyday, nonprofessional lives. We don't have much in the way of "ethical intuitions" to bring to these situations, because we don't encounter these kinds of contractual relationships in the world in which we grow up and receive most of our exposure to ethical norms.

Article 16 of the Realtor® Code of Ethics is simple and straightforward. It reads:

> Realtors® shall not engage in any practice or take any action inconsistent with exclusive representation or exclusive brokerage relationship agreements that other Realtors® have with their clients.

Not surprisingly, such simplicity can lead to questions and misunderstandings. "What about this?" "What about that?" Hence, there are twenty Standards of Practice associated with Article 16, more than are provided for any other Code of Ethics article.

Some have suggested that Article 16 isn't even needed, because it is replicated in the law anyway.[36] This opinion is based on the mistaken belief that a violation of Article 16 is simply a commission of *wrongful interference with a prospective economic advantage*, which in the law is a tort, a wrongful act for which damages can be sought. Such a viewpoint is mistaken on two counts:

(1) Many, perhaps most, cases that would be a violation of Article 16 do not contain all the elements that are required to constitute actionable interference with a prospective economic advantage. Especially relevant is the fact that, to meet this test, the defendant's conduct must be "'wrongful' by some measure beyond the fact of the interference itself."[37]

(2) The viewpoint simply does not take into account the variety of applications of Article 16 that are spelled out in its supplemental Standards of Practice.

---

[36] See, for example, George Mantor, "Can Ethics be Taught?" *Realty Times*, April 5, 2007.

[37] From *Stevenson Real Estate Services v. CB Richard Ellis Real Estate Services, et al.* California's Second Appellate District Court of Appeal, filed April 26, 2006.

If Article 16 doesn't simply repeat what is already in the law, what, then, is its purpose? Perhaps the most complete answer to this question has been given in a paper published by the National Association of Realtors®:

> Competition among brokers to provide appraising, brokerage, managing, leasing, syndicating, or counseling services is extremely intense until the prospective client enters into a binding agreement for such services. When an exclusive relationship is created, the competition shifts to the search for buyers or to otherwise fulfill the agreement. At this point Article 16 comes into play.
>
> Once clients have selected a particular broker to serve their interests, the competition that prevailed earlier ceases and cooperation takes its place.
>
> The client has made a decision and is entitled to the benefit of his or her bargain. This includes *relief for the duration of the relationship from direct overtures of other Realtors®* seeking to interest the seller or lessor in the services they provide. [38] [my emphasis]

In short, the chief benefit that Article 16 provides to the consumer is relief, relief from being solicited. This is no small thing.

Article 16 is not the only Code of Ethics article that governs a Realtor®'s relations with other Realtors®. Another is Article 15, which is both commonly invoked and easily misunderstood. [39] Article 15 states:

> Realtors® shall not knowingly or recklessly make false or misleading statements about competitors, their businesses, or their business practices.

---

[38] *Professionalism in Real Estate Practice*, © 2000 National Association of Realtors®.

[39] Also grouped under the heading "Duties to Realtors®" is Article 17, which is largely concerned with arbitration and procedural matters.

It is sometimes thought that this article prohibits Realtors® from making critical comments about the business practices of another Realtor®, but that is not the case. The focus of the article is on the making of false or misleading statements. It is no violation of the Code of Ethics to be critical, as long as one speaks the truth.

Postdated Listing

You couldn't really feel sorry for Jake. After all, he was probably the most successful real estate agent in town, if not the whole county. The mere fact that someone else beat him out on a listing did not exactly mean that hard times lay ahead.

Still, you could have some sympathy for someone so competitive. Jake was one of those agents who absolutely dominated the five neighborhoods that he farmed. He did everything by the book; he did it right; and no one worked harder. His efforts had paid off handsomely. But still, at the end of the day, if someone else's sign went up in his farm, it just killed him.

Not that he had anything against Rich. Rich was an excellent agent, and Jake respected him, even liked him. Be that as it may, when Rich listed the Barons' house on Avendon Lane, Jake fell into his ritual of remorse. "How could they list with Rich? I sell five times as many houses as he does. And I've sold four on Avendon; he's never even sold one in the tract, for crying out loud!"

It probably wouldn't even have mattered if Jake had known the details of what had happened. Rich didn't "beat him out of the listing" as if they had competed. There had never been a contest. Rich's wife and Mrs. Baron were sorority sisters. Case closed.

Thus, even though Jake took no pleasure in the fact that the market had become rather sluggish, at least there was a silver lining to the economic cloud: The Barons' house hadn't sold. As a matter of fact, he was to find out later, it was over two months into the listing period, and they hadn't even had an offer.

It seemed odd after all those years of knocking on doors and talking to the owners that now Jake never called on the Barons. Tom Baron even remarked to his wife that he felt shunned to see Jake's annual Fourth of July flags planted in all the neighbors' lawns, but not in theirs. It was as if they had been labeled unpatriotic.

But that was just because Jake was a by-the-book kind of guy. He didn't even want the appearance of soliciting the listing of someone who had currently engaged the services of another Realtor®.

Of course, Jake couldn't, and wouldn't, ignore Tom Baron calling to him from the driveway. Jake was just making his way down the front walk of number 131, next door on the left, when he heard Tom's voice. "Jake, come on over here. We've missed talking to you. It's not like we have a communicable disease or something, just because we are listed with one of your competitors."

Tom's invitation was hard to resist, and why resist it anyway? It was Tom, not Jake, who initiated the contact, and there was no soliciting going on. Besides, Jake actually did like the Barons and was happy to reconnect with them.

Judy was inside, and that gave Tom more freedom to speak. He told Jake the story of how they came to list with Rich.

"Tom, you don't have to explain that to me, though I do appreciate it. Anyway, Rich is a fine agent. You can put your confidence in him."

"That's good of you to say, Jake," Tom replied, "but I don't think he's as good as you are. And I know he doesn't understand and know how to sell this neighborhood the way you do."

"Well, really, Tom ..." Jake began, but he was cut off.

"Jake, I'm just plain not satisfied. I told Judy when this started that Rich would get one chance and one chance only. Our listing period only has two weeks left to run, and we have had no activity at all. Come inside with me, I want to show you what kind of advertising Rich has done, and I want you to talk to Judy about what you can do."

Jake, being a true professional, always carried a basic set of contracts with him. Hence, when he emerged from the Barons' house, he carried with him a fully executed listing agreement, to take effect two weeks hence, the day after Rich's listing would expire.

Postdated Listing: Comments and Analysis

In my experience, a large proportion of Realtors® who encounter a story like this are inclined to think that Jake's behavior was entirely out of line. They will say that he should not have talked business with the Barons when they were listed with a competitor, and he certainly had no business taking a postdated listing. As a matter of fact, though, that opinion is mistaken; at least it is mistaken as far as the Realtor® Code of Ethics is concerned.

Standard of Practice 16-6 applies to postdated listings:

> When Realtors® are contacted by the client of another Realtor® regarding the creation of an exclusive relationship to provide the same type of service, and Realtors® have not directly or indirectly initiated such discussions, they may discuss the terms upon which they might enter into a future agreement or, alternatively, *may enter into an agreement which becomes effective upon expiration of any existing exclusive agreement.* [my emphasis]

Jake had been extremely careful not to do anything that could be construed as even indirectly initiating a discussion about a future listing agreement with the Barons. It was Tom Baron who approached Jake and wanted to talk to him about his dissatisfaction and his interest in Jake's future service. Once they had started down that road, it was perfectly legitimate for Jake to take the postdated listing. That this is OK often comes as a surprise to Realtors®, especially conscientious Realtors®.

Curiously, the profession has done such a good job of emphasizing what sometimes seems to be thought of as the "sanctity" of the agency relationship that often it is misconstrued. Some Realtors® occasionally appear to think that it would be a violation for another Realtor® ever to even talk about *any* real estate matter with a person who is currently another agent's principal in an agency relationship. That just isn't so.

It would have been wrong—a clear violation of Article 16—if Jake had initiated the discussion, that is, if he had *solicited* the listing. And this isn't just a technical issue as to who said the first words. If Tom had engaged Jake in a conversation about baseball, and Jake had subsequently turned the conversation to the listing issue, then it would still be considered a solicitation; and Jake would be in violation.

Frequently, it may well be difficult to ascertain whether Article 16 has been violated or whether there was truly an exception under Standard of Practice 16-6. Under the best of circumstances, it isn't easy to reconstruct how a conversation flowed. It's one thing to know what the Standard of Practice says; it's something else to determine what happened in a particular case.

The point, though, remains clear. If it had been the principal's intent to discuss the creation of a future representation agreement, then it is perfectly acceptable for the Realtor® to have that conversation and even to execute a postdated agreement.

Exclusive Representation

It was true: A bad day fishing *is* better than a good day at work. So George thought, as he pointed the boat back to the harbor. He and Mike didn't have much to show for their efforts—just a couple of barely legal bass that wouldn't even be enough to feed the families fish tacos that evening. But it sure beat working. It was a fabulous day; and being out on the water like that—with cell phones off—seemed like he was off on vacation.

Of course, maybe he *was* working. After all, in the years that George and Joanne and Mike and Anita had known each other, it was sometimes hard to tell the difference between business and pleasure. It had started with a real estate transaction, but then they went on to become close friends. Over the years, George had represented Mike and Anita in literally dozens of real estate deals. They were always talking about this deal or that—when they were at dinner, after the movies, or at a kid's ball game. Work, if you could call it "work," kind of permeated their relationship. But their friendship was sincere.

"What do you think, Mike?" George asked as he handed over a beer. "Do we stop at the fish market on the way home?"

Mike laughed and nodded, "I guess so, buddy. We did promise to supply the taco filling tonight. Unless you want to pick up a can of refried beans. The kids always go for that."

"So, my friend, tell me what you think about selling the triplex. Are you getting any calls or inquiries? I thought it would sell pretty quick, but it's been two months now. Do you think we need to lower the price?"

"No, I don't think so, Mike. This has been a little bit of a strange season for investment property. You know how it is: When the stock market begins to run up, then people forget about what a good investment real estate is. But they'll be back, and I don't think it will be long. The Dow is due for a big correction. And there are a lot of good real estate opportunities around here."

"Amen to that, brother," said Mike. "In fact, I had been meaning to tell you that I was able to get into one of those new buildings out in the industrial park. It hasn't closed escrow yet, but we'll do that within the next couple of weeks. I'll tell you, that's going to be a moneymaker. I've already been approached about a lease."

Fortunately, George was at the wheel, with his sunglasses on, looking away from Mike, so Mike wasn't able to see just how wide George's eyes could get. "You bought one of those buildings? I thought they had all been sold even before construction started."

"Yes, they were, but something happened to the deal on this one. Anyway, your friend, Letisha Williams—remember, she brought us an offer on the last house we sold—called me and told me about it. I guess she knew the developer. She had this 'pocket listing,' or whatever it's called, and she was able to slip me right in and take the place of the previous buyer. It's going to be a terrific deal."

The rest of the trip back was uneventful. George never showed what he was feeling. They picked up some more fish on the way home. The two families enjoyed fish tacos and called it an evening. What a great day.

Letisha's phone rang early the next morning. It was George. "What the hell do you think you are doing, poaching on my client like that?"

"George ..." she began, but he cut her off.

"Damn it, Letisha, we've been friends for a long time, but this is just outrageous. You know that Mike and Anita Dahlstrom have been my clients for years. Not only that, you know that I have an exclusive listing on his triplex right now. What did you think you were doing, approaching him about that commercial building? That's the most unethical thing I've ever heard of!"

Letisha tried again, "George, the commercial building had nothing to do with your triplex listing. It was a good deal, and I remembered what an investor he was, so I called him. You don't *own* him, George."

"I just can't believe you, Letisha, interfering with my agency like that. I'll be seeing you at the ethics hearing."

Exclusive Representation: Comments and Analysis

Especially in cases where a Realtor® has dealt with the same client in more than a couple of transactions, a feeling of what we might call "persistent agency" may form. When things go well, relationships may develop that make Realtors® feel that they are the principals' "agent for life." The principals may even feel that way too. That is partly what is going on in "Exclusive Representation," and Letisha hits the nail on the head with her final comment: "You don't *own* him, George." An agency relationship ends when the object of the agency is achieved. It might be a purchase, a lease, or a sale, but when it is over, it is over. (Though some of the obligations attendant to the agency—such as the obligation to preserve confidential information—may persist even beyond its termination.)

George is incorrect to think that Letisha has acted unethically because she contacted his client about *buying* a property during the time that George was his *listing* agent on another property. Standard of Practice 16-3 is quite explicit about this:

> Article 16 does not preclude Realtors® from contacting the client of another broker for the purpose of offering to provide, or entering into a contract to provide, *a different type of real estate service unrelated to the type of service currently being provided* (e.g. property management as opposed to brokerage) or from offering the same type of service for property not subject to other brokers' exclusive agreements. However, information received through a Multiple Listing Service or any other offer of cooperation may not be used to target clients of other Realtors® to whom such offers to provide services may be made. [*my emphasis*]

First of all, Letisha was offering a service unrelated to the type of service that George was currently providing under an exclusive agreement. Secondly, she had not "targeted" George's client, Mike, on the basis of information gleaned from the Multiple Listing Service. Rather, she approached him on the basis of information she had acquired in an earlier relationship. What she did was perfectly acceptable under the Realtor® Code of Ethics. George may want to file a complaint with the Grievance Committee, but it shouldn't go very far.

We also note, looking at the Standard of Practice, that it would have been legitimate for Letisha to contact Mike to seek to obtain a listing on some other property that Mike owned (but that was not currently listed with George or anyone else). She would have been offering the same type of service that George was currently providing, but not on the same property.

It's fairly easy to see how this Standard of Practice benefits the consumer, in this case the seller. While the general stricture of Article 16 is useful to protect a seller from being bombarded with solicitations, it is not the intent of the article that the principal be denied the opportunity of learning about other potentially beneficial real estate opportunities.

Bad Blogging

Doug was actually surprised that his neighborhood website had been such a marketing help. For years he and Justin had slugged it out—figuratively speaking—competing with all the traditional farming methods. They both mailed newsletters, walked the neighborhood, sent out "Just Listed" and "Just Sold" cards. They each held promotional events—from handing out Halloween pumpkins to providing "spring cleaning" dumpsters. They pretty much did it all, and they had remained remarkably even in market share.

Then came the neighborhood website. What a great idea! Of all the vendor product presentations he had suffered listening to at office meetings, this one was the best. It actually made sense. A website devoted to the neighborhood: It contained floorplans, all the listed and sold activity, links to the school district, garage sale notices, babysitting services, and on and on. The vendor provided the shell and showed Doug how to add and modify, and Doug provided the information. Best of all, it was exclusive—only one real estate agent per farm area.

It took a while to get off the ground, but word of mouth had its effect. (What a wonderful irony, Doug thought: the most effective way to advertise his state-of-the-art web service was by old-fashioned word of mouth.) And though it wasn't yet clear that the website had brought him any significant lead in market share, it sure was helping his bottom line. Everything he used to do by mail—all those expensive, glossy pieces—he could now put up on the website. He still mailed, of course, but to a greatly reduced list at a greatly reduced cost. Almost

60% of his target group had told him—via the site—that they were using the site, and he didn't need to bother with snail mail.

Recently, one of his clients suggested that Doug start a blog on the website. Doug would post a commentary or opinion on some topic or another, then his readers could post their reactions and comments to his thoughts, others could react to *those* comments, and everyone could see what everyone had said. Its interactive, "everyone participates" nature reminded him of the old online community bulletin boards. It was just unbelievable to him how many people wanted to express their opinions on just about every topic under the sun.

One of the most recent discussions focused on the subject of *professionalism in real estate*. Doug had written a little piece giving his thoughts. Little did he know that he would be stirring up a hornet's nest. At first he was almost dumbfounded by all the bad real estate experiences people had had. The discussion had almost begun to take on a "can you top this?" atmosphere.

Doug had been online only for a few minutes when he came upon the most recent posting. It was about Justin. And it was ugly.

"Honey, come look at this," he called to Peggy. She did. "Oh, Doug, is this true?"

"No, I don't believe it is. At least it's not the way I heard it. As I remember, the previous owners had covered up a really serious problem. But Justin, who was the listing agent, didn't know, and he couldn't have been expected to discover it on his own. Anyway, he and his company were dismissed out of the case. And their E&O insurance was the only deep pocket available. The home inspector went BK; and the sellers had actually left the country. The court couldn't reach them.

"So, it cost the buyers—the Culligans—a lot of money, and they always blamed Justin."

"What are you going to do about this?"

"Frankly, I'm not sure; that's partly why I called you over. I'm inclined to just leave it. First of all, the blog has been going just great; and I don't think I want to start censoring what people say. That could kill it. Second, people like the Culligans are going to go ahead and say what they say, anyway. I know their nearby neighbors have already had an earful. Finally, and I really am concerned about this, if I cut them off, what are they going to start saying about *me?*"

"I see your point, Doug, and you do have good ground to stand on. I mean 'freedom of the press'—'freedom of the blog.' It's all very democratic. I agree; you ought to leave it. Besides, people have a way of sorting out what is true anyway."

Bad Blogging: Comments and Analysis

Article 15 of the Realtor® Code of Ethics says simply:

> Realtors® shall not knowingly or recklessly make false or misleading statements about competitors, their businesses, or their business practices.

Many people take that to mean that Realtors® are not to *disparage* their competitors or their competitors' business practices. But that is not what the article says. The article refers to false or misleading statements. However, it's possible that one could disparage the practices of another—that is, speak of them critically, belittle them, or even ridicule them—without saying anything that was either false or misleading. If that were the case, it would not be a violation of Article 15.

The Preamble to the Realtor® Code of Ethics, which is held to describe behaviors to which Realtors® should aspire, but which are not necessarily their *duties*, says the following:

> [Realtors®] refrain from making unsolicited comments about other practitioners. In instances where their opinion is sought, or where Realtors® believe that comment is necessary, their opinion is offered in an

> objective, professional manner, uninfluenced by any
> personal motivation or potential advantage or gain.

Even with this more broadly stated injunction, saying critical things about another's business practices, in some circumstances, clearly may be tolerated, as long as what is said is true.

Of course, in general it may be bad manners or undesirable behavior to speak critically of other persons. "If you can't say something nice, don't say nothin' at all" was the advice of Thumper's father in *Bambi*, and it's not a bad rule to follow; but it probably falls short of an ethical obligation. Especially if some third party needs to be warned about the actual bad behavior of another.

Saying something that is false or misleading (which may be just as bad as false) is another matter. Indeed, this would be one of those instances where we could just rely on general ethical principles. It's dishonest to say false and/or misleading things, and it is wrong. We knew that even without the Realtor® Code of Ethics.[40]

But what about *other people* saying something false or misleading about someone? It would be implausible to say that, generally, we have an obligation to keep others from engaging in such behavior. For the most part, we don't have the means or the duty to act as "ethics police" when it comes to others. We would, though, if our children were the perpetrators; and we could probably think of some extreme cases where someone's gossip or false disparagement might be so hurtful that *we* should step in and stop it.

In any event, we certainly shouldn't knowingly repeat false things said by others. And that is what Standard of Practice 15-2 makes clear:

> The obligation to refrain from making false or mislead-

---

[40] I am indebted to Cliff Niersbach of NAR for pointing out to me that the article also prohibits saying false things that, rather than being disparaging, might be complimentary or positive. Although occasions where this might happen would appear to be unlikely, it is certainly a possibility. Imagine "puffing" an agent to whom one was giving a referral and saying untruthfully to the client, "Oh, yes, she is one of the top-producing agents in the area."

ing statements about competitors' businesses and competitors' business practices includes the duty to not knowingly or recklessly repeat, retransmit, or republish false or misleading statements made by others. This duty applies whether false or misleading statements are repeated in person, in writing, *by technological means (e.g. the Internet),* or by any other means. [*my emphasis*]

Not only does the Standard make clear that we ought not to repeat false disparaging things said by others, it also makes clear that we ought not to allow that to happen by means of communications methods that are within our control. This Standard of Practice was adopted only recently, and it is a clear example of adjusting and modifying the Code in order to keep it applicable to current situations and technologies.[41]

The Internet provides a powerful, and therefore potentially dangerous, vehicle for passing along the thoughts of others. Anyone who looks at e-mail can attest to the myriad of warnings, alerts, and alleged "news scoops" that get passed along by well-intentioned, if not critically thinking, friends, relatives, and acquaintances. It is staggering how many unfounded and/or false reports are passed on. It is also staggering how many people believe them.

While it may be just generally irresponsible to pass along sensational stories without having any idea whether they are true, it is ethically unacceptable to pass along stories we know to be false. In the context of the real estate business, it is a violation of the Realtor® Code of Ethics. In the context of our story, Doug is going to need to exercise some editorial responsibility for what is posted on his blog.

---

[41] I should note that my conclusion here—that under Standard of Practice 15-2, Realtors® would have a duty to edit or censor false statements by others that are posted to the Realtor®'s blog—is a personal interpretation that has not yet been specifically supported by the Professional Standards Committee of NAR.

10

Agent-Broker Relations

For purposes of these discussions the term *broker* is being used in a somewhat restricted way. It doesn't simply refer to "anyone who holds a broker license." Nor would it necessarily apply to a person who might legally be registered as the broker of a large multi-office company but who, in fact, may have nothing to do with the policies or day-to-day operations of the company. Here, we want to talk about the person (or persons) who is involved with the company practices and who is the ultimate determiner of its operational policies. In some cases this could be a branch manager who does not even possess a broker license. Typically, though, it will be an owner-broker, actively involved in the on-going business of the company.

Real estate workplaces vary widely. Usually, agents are independent contractors, but in many circumstances, the relationship between broker and agent seems more like that of employer-employee. Moreover, there are some companies where employer-employee actually *is* the legal relationship. Not only is there what we might call this *functional* variation between agent and broker, there is also a *relational* variation. Some companies operate like partnerships; the atmosphere is definitely "we're all in this together." Others have a much more labor-management style, and sometimes that can even deteriorate to an "us versus them" situation.

It is not the aim of this text to advocate one functional model over another, but it is to make clear that, whether a brokerage characterizes itself as a "family" or whether it is "strictly business," the same ethical considerations apply with respect to the relationships between brokers and their agents. Just as real estate firms owe it to the public and to their clients to be truthful, they also have such an obligation to their agents. And agents owe the same to the firm as well. In every contractual relationship there is an implied covenant of good faith and fair dealing. This applies to the relationship between brokers and their agents as much as it does to them and their clients. Sad to say, this is not always honored. It should be.

Whether a firm styles itself as a "partnership," a "family," or a "strictly business" operation, it is a given that the well-being of the company and the well-being of the agents are inextricably intertwined. There may be some short-term exceptions to this; for a while an agent may thrive while the company is in serious trouble, or vice versa. However, over the long term their fortunes are tied together.

Moreover, the interrelationship of the company and the agents is not simply restricted to financial results. It applies to reputation and character as well. Brokers need to be concerned about the ethics of their agents. That is widely acknowledged. Less recognized is the fact that agents need to be equally concerned about the ethics of their brokers. For both, this is not just a concern about the financial bottom line or about how one is liable to be treated. It has to do with how one's character is influenced and formed by association and about how we are known by the company we keep.

Share the Wealth

It was a great party, but Cindy may have had just a tad too much to drink. She was talking out of school. "Really, Nick, this is the way it goes down. Frank's version of 'sharing the wealth' is that he gets all the good stuff, and the rest of you guys can fight over the crumbs."

"Cindy, you are a sweetheart, and I appreciate you one hundred percent, but let's not talk about this anymore tonight. I'll call you first part of next week, and you can tell me then whatever you want to tell me. Right now," Nick cautioned, "we should just talk party talk."

Frank's Together Realty franchise office (officially: *Together Realty Frank Martin and Associates*, "Each Office Independently Owned and Operated") was the kind of success story that made his operation a franchise poster child. Frank had been a moderately successful broker in Small Creek for more than twenty years. In a town of about thirty thousand, he consistently had about sixteen agents on staff. Not the largest company around, but one of the more significant ones.

It was just two years ago that he made the franchise move, but what timing—some might say luck. When he decided to go with the Together Realty franchise, he knew that TZI was moving its headquarters and chief manufacturing facility to Small Creek. That had been in the works for some time. What he didn't know—and, at the time, the franchise reps didn't know it either—was that Together Realty would land the relocation package for the TZI move.

Did that help recruiting, or what? Frank, himself, came up with the "Share the Wealth" theme for his recruiting campaign. The franchise people then did a lot of the support work. The pitch was simple: TZI will be moving to Small Creek. Together Realty is its relocation agent. Whom do you want to be working for when they start to arrive? Frank now had twenty-eight agents, with the prospect of more.

Nick and Cindy sat at a corner table, well removed from the sight or hearing of anyone else who happened to be lunching at The Grille that day. "OK, Cindy, now if you want to elaborate on what you began to tell me at the party—you know, the stuff about sharing the wealth— well, please go ahead."

"I do want to tell you, Nick, because it's been bugging me for some time now." Cindy let out a prolonged sigh, as if a weight had just been lifted from her shoulders. "Nick, you know that one of my titles in the office is Relocation Coordinator—along with Frank's Secretary, Receptionist, Emptier of Waste Baskets, Maker of Coffee, etc. And everybody has been told that I receive the relocation referrals from corporate, and that I then pass them on to agents on a rotation basis, and that the rotation was the result of a random drawing."

"Right, we all know that's one of your many jobs."

"Well, Nick, it doesn't work that way. I don't make the relocation assignments, and they certainly don't go by a 'rotation.' Frank has his hand in every one of them. I give him all the information, and then he makes the decision as to who gets what. You wouldn't know, because he doesn't put his production on the board—you know, the broker shouldn't be able to win the prizes, etc.—but he cherry-picks the really nice ones. Nothing but the TZI executives.

"Now, the other ones—middle managers and the like—he does distribute around pretty evenly, though every now and then he'll give a slam-dunk buyer to one of the weaker agents, like Andy for instance, because he knows the deal will get done, and the agent is on a lower split. More money winds up in Frank's pocket.

"Nick, have you ever wondered why *you* never got any really good TZI buyers? It's because Frank thinks the high producers like you aren't really depending on the referrals, and when you get the impression that they aren't all that good anyway, then you'll just be content to do what you usually do."

"You've got that right, Cindy. I've been doing just fine in Frank's office for years. Sure, that TZI stuff sounded pretty exciting; but then, on the basis of the ones I got, I decided it really wasn't such a big deal. Heck, sometimes I even pass them on to some other agent.

"But what you're telling me has me disturbed. Really disturbed."

Share the Wealth: Comments and Analysis

Brokers engage in favoritism—unequal treatment of agents—in a variety of ways: company-generated leads are distributed unevenly, some agents get better split deals than others, some may have expenses subsidized when others do not, and some may get more and better ad space than others. The list could go on and on.

Brokers have every right to do so. Neither the law nor ethics prohibits this kind of unequal treatment. Moreover, some think that such behavior is good business and that it helps to make a company more profitable.

But no broker has an ethical right, though it may be legal, to *mislead* his agents about the unequal treatment. It doesn't take an ethical genius to know this. The broker who tells his agents that everyone is subject to the same commission-split schedule, but who then cuts special deals with some agents, isn't "exercising entrepreneurial flexibility"—or however one might want to dress it up—he's just plain lying. And that is wrong.

It's not only wrong; it is also shortsighted. It has been noted that companies have better retention rates when employees perceive their bosses to be persons of integrity. There is a reason for this. It was all explained at the 2004 convention of the National Association of Realtors® in Orlando, Florida, in a talk given by Tom Morris.

Tom Morris is a philosopher, not your typical convention speaker; but when he spoke at NAR, it was clear that he knew his audience well. This is not just because the former Notre Dame professor is familiar with business people, having addressed hundreds of corporate seminars and retreats around the country. More important, in this case, is the fact that Tom Morris possesses a North Carolina real estate broker's license. He grew up in a real estate family.

The title of his talk to the Realtors®, reflecting his grounding in the classics, was "If Aristotle Sold Real Estate: The Four Foundations of Excellence." Morris' message, primarily directed to brokers, owners, and managers, is one from the Ancients: Human beings seek fulfillment, and an activity or relationship can contribute to one's fulfillment if and only if it respects and nurtures one of the four fundamental dimensions of human experience. Those dimensions are the Intellectual, the Aesthetic, the Moral, and the Spiritual.

A company or organization that ignores those aspects of its members' experience does so at its peril. Conversely, companies that attend to those factors see payoffs in loyalty, retention, morale, and productivity. It is a lesson for ABC Realty as much as it is a lesson for General Motors.

"Well, OK," a sincere and attentive broker-owner might say, "but just

what does all this stuff mean in the everyday world of my office?
Exactly what might I do to apply these lessons from the ancients?" A
fair enough question; and here, it is relevant to consider the answer as
it bears on the first of the four dimensions.

As Morris would put it, the intellectual dimension of human experience aims at the truth. People have a natural desire to know and to
understand. To satisfy this desire, they need the truth. And, while no
particular environment can supply them with all the truth there is,
every environment can provide an atmosphere of respect for the truth.
People—yes, even real estate agents—have a deep-seated need for this,
and they will not be able to find real satisfaction in an enterprise
where the truth is held in low regard.

Real estate companies, as well as other organizations, can apply this in
at least two ways. Externally, a high regard for the truth will manifest
itself in the way a company presents itself and interacts with both the
general public and its clients.

Internally, they must speak the truth to their employees and agents. At
a minimum, this means no dishonesty. Taken more actively, it means
openness. It means sharing with employees the truth about company
policies, plans and goals, and, especially, problems. It means not
making secret deals with some agents while deceiving the rest. It
doesn't require that every agent gets the same commission split or that
all agents receive leads equally, but it does require that there be no
deception about company policies in those regards.

Broker's Affiliated Business

The decision to form a mortgage company was not a difficult one for
Ben. Although he owned one of the largest (with sixty-two agents) and
most successful brokerages in town, he felt the pinch on broker
profitability just like everyone else. And being an independent, he
didn't have the built-in ancillary services—and concomitant profits—
that some of his "big name" competitors did. Besides, he could see the

handwriting on the wall. Consumers wanted one-stop shopping, and brokers needed to develop profit centers beyond their core business.

Then there was also the aspect that Jason's proposal was something no sane businessman could refuse. Jason's company, Big Rock Mortgage, had already established a presence in the Great River area. In addition to twelve stand-alone offices, they had set up joint ventures (with real estate brokers) in Springdale, McClintock, and East Arlington. It was only natural that they would seek a presence in Clarendon, and from that it followed that they would come knocking at Ben's door.

Who could resist the deal that Jason was proposing? There would be no start-up costs for Ben. Big Rock would fund all the initial outlay and the first three months of expenses. The salary of the loan officer and an assistant as needed would also be borne by Big Rock. Finally, Big Rock would, on behalf of the joint-venture entity, rent that now-vacant office in Ben's building, adjacent to the brokerage and with a common entry, at a price that turned out to be approximately three times fair market value.

The ownership would be 25-75, with the majority held by Big Rock, of course. Dividends would be paid quarterly, and Ben would receive a 10% dividend bonus paid on the number of referrals made to the joint venture.

So, now everything was in place, and the time had come to roll out this new addition to Ben's brokerage business. Only one question remained: How to get the agents to use the new mortgage company?

Most of the agents in Ben's company were seasoned. Forty-three of them averaged seventeen years' real estate experience in the greater Clarendon area. Only eight had less than one year's experience in the business. Agents like the ones at Ben's office already had enjoyed established relationships with those in affiliated services. Many of them had been using their favorite lenders for ten years or more.

It's hard enough to get a real estate agent to change any of his or her habits. How was Ben supposed to get his agents to shake loose from their established lender relations and to use his newly formed mortgage company? He knew that once they got used to it, they would see the value and see how it paid off for the company—and thus indirectly for them. But how to get it started? Ben was well aware that it was illegal to incentivize (should we say, "bribe"?) them by offering referral fees.

As always, Jason had an answer. He had done it before in the other offices, and it always worked. "Here's what we do: We have a contest of sorts, like a drawing or a raffle. First, we guarantee the agents that their clients will receive the same or better rates and costs than any of their previous lenders can offer. We'll stick by that, too, as long as they bring in a bona fide written commitment from the other lender. Then, for every borrower they bring in—make it for the first two months, that's plenty—they will get an entry into our drawing. And it will be big. Maybe an all-expense-paid trip to Hawaii for the winner and a couple of shorter Las Vegas trips for second and third winners.

"These agents know we can't compensate them for referrals, but this is different. In a drawing, no one particularly wins on the basis of what they have referred. And the awards of benefits are different. The winners can't tie their prizes to any particular loan that they referred."

Ben announced the "contest," and it was received enthusiastically. The mortgage company was up and running in a flash. The agents were excited. Someone was going to Hawaii.

Broker's Affiliated Business: Comments and Analysis

Ben's analysis of his situation is right on. Consumers do want one-stop shopping, and the difficulty in providing that puts a competitive squeeze on independent small to mid-size brokers. He's right about the second part too. Despite what the Federal Trade Commission and *Sixty Minutes* might think, there continues to be strong, competition-driven downward pressure on brokerage commissions. Moreover, brokers are caught in the middle of that, on the one hand, and, on the other, the competition-driven pressure to give higher commission splits to their agents. There is simply less return to be earned on brokerage services, and brokers need to look to the establishment of profit centers beyond their core business.

The creation of an affiliated business arrangement (ABA, sometimes also referred to as AfBA) through a joint venture is a natural attempt to address these issues. A 2004 white paper prepared by the Legal Affairs Department of the National Association of Realtors® says this:

> Section 8(a) of RESPA prohibits giving or receiving fees or kickbacks for the referral of settlement service business involving a federally-related mortgage loan. See 12 U.S.C. §2607(a). There is a statutory exemption for affiliated business arrangements that allows referrals to an affiliated settlement service provider under certain circumstances. *An affiliated business arrangement is an arrangement in which a person (such as a real estate broker or agent) is in a position to refer settlement business to a settlement service provider that is owned, in whole or in part, by the referring party.* 12 U.S.C. §2607(c). Under this arrangement, the referring party receives no direct payment for the referral to the settlement service provider in which he has an ownership interest, but he can receive indirect compensation based on the financial growth of the affiliated provider.[42] [*my emphasis*]

An important point in determining whether or not an ABA is properly structured has to do with the manner in which payments are made to the ownership entities.

> To qualify for the affiliated business arrangement exemption the referring party may receive payments only in the form of a return on ownership interest. See Statement of Policy, Fed. Reg. at 29262. A return on ownership interest does not include (1) payments that vary by the amount of actual, estimated or anticipated

---

[42] *How HUD Determines Whether a Mortgage or Title Company Is a Sham*, NAR, 2004. For HUD's tests for determining whether an ABA is formed properly, see Appendix 1.

referrals; or (2) payments based on ownership shares
adjusted on the basis of previous referrals.[43]

Ben's ABA did not meet that test, because he was to receive a bonus
based on the number of referrals that were made.

There were other tests that Ben's venture did not meet as well. It is left
to the reader to look at the HUD tests in Appendix 1 and to try to
figure what at least some of the other issues were.

There was also a problem with the contest. It doesn't matter that the
prize itself was not tied to any particular loan or any particular agent's
production. The prize was not the only thing of value at issue. Entries
into a contest are, themselves, things of value, and in this case they
were being given in return for loans referred. They were given in direct
proportion to the referrals, which is a clear RESPA violation.

None of this is said to condemn Ben or his real-life counterparts.
Many brokers and agents are in the same position as are many affiliates. They just don't know; and they see so many examples of companies and individuals engaging in activities that are, in fact, prohibited
that sometimes it is hard for them to believe that all those things could
be violations. But in these instances, ignorance is not bliss. It is better
to become acquainted with these rules than it is to learn them as the
result of a HUD investigation.

Agents have a role to play in this too. After all, more than a few of the
questionable programs brokers and affiliates may engage in are ones
that are designed to make the agents happy (and, therefore, to stay
with the broker). Agents owe it to their brokers, if they really want to
be a part of a right-acting company, to express to them their concerns
about any programs or activities that they feel may be wrong. These
things should be talked about at the office level. Surprising things
could happen. A broker could likely be relieved to find out that he
doesn't have to participate in a RESPA-violating scheme just to please
his agents. He might please them by *not* doing so.

---

[43] From the same paper.

| Moles |

The HT&T Realty office had been open for about six weeks now. It would be fair to say that none of the town's established brokerages were particularly happy to see yet another new franchise come into town. Who knew what kind of song and dance and promises they would use to try to lure away experienced agents! Though, for the moment, at least, no one was feeling terribly threatened. The new office had hardly opened with a bang. It was more like a fizzle. To the delight of the local brokers, HT&T had so far filled only eight desks at their brand new 3500 square-foot facility.

Little did they know.

"Welcome to another Friday night meeting of the Secret Society," said Emily, as Juan took a seat next to Alexis. "It looks like this might be our last meeting before making the switch. Ryan says we've reached critical mass. It's time to do it."

"That'll be OK with me," Juan responded. "In a way, it's been kind of fun, but I don't think I was cut out for this secrecy stuff. I never could have been a CIA agent."

"Don't worry," Alexis kidded, "you can turn in your trench coat pretty soon. But, let's get down to business. Recruiting report, please."

"Well, my total stands at six," Emily chimed in. I only picked up one more—Olivia Cantwell—this week. She is excited, though."

"I'm at seven," said Juan, "On Wednesday, both Lauren Black and Tyler Redding let me know that they wanted in on the ground floor. They're excited too. I think the meeting with Ryan was the clincher."

"You pikers," laughed Alexis. "I added another six this week. That makes fourteen total for me. Am I going to get the recruiter of the month award, or what?"

"Six more? Get out! How did you ever do *that?*"

"Oh, I wish I could concoct some story about my super techniques, but actually, I didn't really do anything. Good old broker Bob did it for me: He announced that our E&O renewal would be next month, and of course the rates are higher. Everyone is going to have to pony up $1,200 on the fifteenth. Well, if you don't think that made the HT&T per-transaction charge look good ... Anyway, put me down for a total of fourteen, and start figuring *my* recruiting bonuses."

"Anybody having problems about leaving business behind?" asked Emily.

"No, not really," responded Juan. "Some of us will have to pay a little to have our existing escrows 'serviced' by one of their agents, but we'll get the bulk of our commissions. Of my three listings, two are set to expire in just a little while anyway—what a coincidence—and then they will re-list with me at the new office. The other one I don't much care to hang onto anyway.

"But let me tell you about the buyers I'm working with," he continued. "This is really rich. They were walk-ins from out of state about two weeks ago. It was late, and I happened to be the only one at the office, so I took them out. We really bonded. Well, when I told them I would be going to HT&T soon, they just about flipped. They're listed with an HT&T office in their hometown. Anyway, I got them in touch with Ryan. He took them out once, but they'll be all mine next week. They're good buyers too."

It all went like clockwork. Desks were emptied and everything moved on Sunday night. Ryan had arranged for three trucks with workers. Licenses were transferred electronically on the Real Estate Department website. Nothing had to be sent in by the brokers whom they were leaving, just by the one where the licenses would now be located.

Come Monday morning, about the same time that three office managers were learning that their ranks had been seriously thinned, HT&T began its weekly meeting. Now thirty-eight strong, the office looked pretty full, and there was a buzz of excitement and anticipation.

"What a pleasure it is to welcome you," Ryan began, "because I am not just welcoming you to a new location, I am welcoming you to a whole new way of doing business in real estate. I know that a lot of you have been in this business for years and that you've experienced a lot of practices that were distasteful. You know of companies where everyone is out for himself, and backstabbing and client-stealing are a way of life. Well, not here. HT&T—honesty, trust, and transparency—are not just slogans here. They are the values we live by and the way we do business. You're going to love it.

"But that's enough speech. Before we get down to business details, let's give a big hand to Alexis, Emily, and Juan—who patiently waited to make the move so that they could encourage you to come with them."

Moles: Comments and Analysis

Just in case it isn't clear, what's going on here is that the three agents—Alexis, Emily, and Juan—have committed to joining HT&T, but before making the move, they are going to remain with their current companies and use that opportunity to recruit on behalf of HT&T. There is a recruiting bonus as an incentive. They aren't just "waiting for the right time" to make the change.

What they are doing is not illegal. It would be a real stretch to try to characterize their behavior as "wrongful interference with a prospective economic advantage," and it surely wouldn't stick in court. Nor is their behavior covered by any sections of the Realtor® Code of Ethics. (Perhaps, though, one might wish that it were.) Nonetheless, their activity can be analyzed from an ethical perspective, and it should be.

Of course there is nothing inherently wrong with leaving one company for another. It happens all the time and under a variety of circumstances. But what about remaining with the original company for a while, so that you can do some recruiting for the company you will be joining?

It is unlikely that such behavior is covered by whatever broker-agent independent contractor (or employment) agreement may be in place. Nor is it likely that this circumstance will be covered in an office policy and procedures manual. Typically, those documents will have some provisions concerning the agent not soliciting clients of the firm or prospective clients that were generated through company leads. However, they are not likely to consider the solicitation of other agents.[44]

If this behavior isn't addressed by the law, or contractually, or under the Code of Ethics, it can still be considered from the perspective of the Golden Rule. If you were the broker, it is pretty clear that you wouldn't want to be treated that way. You wouldn't invite or allow another company's recruiter to use your office space or its relational opportunities, and you certainly wouldn't want your own agents to be exploiting those things.

A persistent "mole" recruiter might respond by saying, "Look, I'm not like someone from the outside. I've paid for these facilities –through my commission splits, or admin fees, or some other arrangement—and, as long as I'm paid up—I have every right to talk about whatever I want." Well, that might be an attempt at a sort-of-legal argument, but it really won't wash ethically. The broker would probably see the recruiting activities as potentially costing him heavily. It's something we wouldn't want done to us if we were in his shoes, and that's a good reason not to do it to him.

We have noted that it is good living as well as good business for a broker to foster a climate of honesty, trust, and transparency (the stated values of HT&T) in his firm. But trust is a two-way street. If someone acts in such a way that you can trust him, you owe that person reciprocal treatment. Agents need to be open and honest with brokers, just as brokers need to be open and honest with agents.

HT&T claimed to be built on great values, but it did a pretty poor job of demonstrating that. Any agent who was aware of the situation

---

[44] In the story, the recruiting activity was compounded by the fact that one of the agents had actually sent a company-generated lead to the firm that he would be joining. Most independent contractor agreements probably aren't written tightly enough to make that actionable, but it was clearly wrong.

would be pretty unlikely to put a lot of faith in the idea that HT&T was going to "walk the talk." The competition among brokers for agents is every bit as intense as the competition among agents for prospects. The same principles apply. An agent needs to behave as ethically in *trying to get a listing* as he is obligated to behave once he has it. Similarly, brokers, along with their agents and employees, need to be as ethical in their recruiting practices as they aspire to be in their brokerage operations.

Afterwords

Afterword 1: How to Become an Ethical Real Estate Agent

Robert Solomon, one of the premier Business Ethics philosophers in the country, writes:

> Whether we do well, whether we like ourselves, whether we lead happy productive lives, depends to a large extent on the companies we choose. As the Greeks used to say, "to live the good life one must live in a great city." To my business students today, who are all too prone to choose a job on the basis of salary and start-up bonus alone, I always say, "to live a decent life, choose the right company."[45]

Do you want to live a decent life, to like yourself as a real estate agent, to be as ethical in your business life as you would be in your personal life? Find a good company. (It should be obvious that we are using "good" here in the sense of *ethically good*. It is probably more common to think of "good agent" and "good company" in terms of productivity. That is important, to be sure, but it is not what we mean here.) How? Look for a company with good people, ethical people.[46] If good people have been attracted to and stayed with a company, that is a good—albeit not perfect—indicator of its ethical climate.

---

[45] Robert Solomon, "Corporate Roles, Personal Virtues: An Aristotelean Approach to Business Ethics," in Donaldson, Werhane, and Cording, *Ethical Issues in Business*, 7th ed., Prentice Hall, 2002, 75.

[46] This may be difficult to do if you are new to the area or new to the business. If that's the case, try asking people in a related business such as escrow, title, and mortgage. They're liable to know and to be willing to tell you.

Look for a company with values. Now just about every real estate company on the planet will tell you that they have and believe in values and high ethical standards, so you may need to dig a little deeper. Ask how they implement those values. Ask what they do to reinforce them. Ask them if they have a plan or a program to instill and support these values.[47]

Hang around with good people. If there are agents in your company who have a reputation for being ethical and decent in the way they conduct their business, try to put yourself in their presence. If someone in your real estate association has that kind of reputation, seek him out. Most agents who have been around this business for a while have heard some trainer suggest to them that they should seek out top producers, take them to lunch, try to learn from them. The same principle applies. "You play better golf with better golfers."

Avoid the bad guys. You can be nice, you can be friendly, but don't make them your regular associates.

Work on developing good habits. If anyone knows that we can change or develop our habits, salespeople do. We can teach ourselves, or be taught, to make all sorts of behaviors (think about prospecting) part of our routines; we internalize scripts to prepare for every manner of objections and situations. Coaches make a living holding us accountable to the development of good business habits. We should bring the same kinds of disciplines and techniques to shape our ethical behavior.

How do we develop habits that will guide us through the maze of ethical decisions and situations we are liable to encounter in our business? By concentrating on what may appear to be "the little things." Tom Morris, the philosopher with a real estate broker license, writes:

---

[47] More than a few interviewers may not have the foggiest idea what you are talking about. That doesn't mean they are bad people. It just suggests that the company's commitment to values may not be terribly strong. If the answer is something like, "Teaching ethics is the job of the board (or, association)," that pretty much indicates the same thing.

Too many people in high places talk big about ethics, and morality, and virtue, and goodness, but do not practice these qualities when they interact day-to-day with the people who work for them. There are far too many people who want to increase the general weal of the world without doing the unglamorous and sometimes inconvenient work of, for example, responding in kindness to a coworker during a time of stress. The little kindnesses, the small decencies, form the foundation for truly magnificent things.[48]

To this he adds:

If I could pass on only one thing I've discovered in the realm of wisdom and virtue, this would be it ...

Whenever you make a decision, whenever you act, you are never just doing, you are always becoming.

... In everything we do, however large or small, we should always be asking ourselves: "In doing this, am I becoming the kind of person I want to be?" One of the greatest dangers in life is the ever-present threat of self-deception. We often believe we can do something, "just this one time," without its having any implications for who we are. But there are no exceptions to this process. We can never take a holiday from moral significance.

Develop the habit of taking others into account, of putting yourself in their shoes. Think about how your actions will affect others; again, put yourself in their shoes. Do this in the so-called "little things" and you'll find your instincts are right when it comes to the big things. Columnist Dave Barry once wrote, "A person who is nice to you, but rude to a waiter, is not a nice person." Tom Morris would agree wholeheartedly. If a real estate office becomes a place where "little acts of kindness" are practiced routinely, where friendliness and cheerfulness are

---

[48] Tom Morris, *If Aristotle Ran General Motors*, New York, Owl Books, Henry Holt & Company, 1998, 164-65.

the norm—and where rudeness and mean-spiritedness are out of place—then the moral dimension of its agents will be nurtured, and they can be expected to do what is right in the "big" situations.

Finally, think about the Realtor® Code of Ethics. I'm not saying memorize it, or read a portion every day, or anything like that. But look at the sections that apply to your situations from time to time. Try to understand why it says what it says. And, if you find yourself puzzled, go find one of those good people and talk about it.

Afterword 2: How to Have an Ethical Real Estate Company

Robert Solomon's advice to those who want to be ethically good businesspeople is "join a good company." There is a corollary to that principle. If you want to have an ethically good company, hire good people. This isn't always an easy thing to do. Sometimes a broker may be fortunate enough to be able to hire an agent who is already well respected in the community, but, frequently, the new or slightly experienced agents who come in the door don't yet have a reputation, for good or for bad. A broker will just have to do the best he or she can.

One thing, though, is for sure: Don't hire people who are known to be bad actors, and don't keep those who are discovered to be. Once again, Tom Morris speaks aptly: "This is why the great thinkers have always encouraged us to avoid bad company. Bad company corrupts. And absolute scoundrels corrupt absolutely." It simply isn't worth it to keep bad apples—no matter how much money they might bring in.

Of course, a broker can do more than just wait and see if new hires turn out to be good people. The broker can be proactive. Tom Morris introduces the notion of *moral mentoring*, which is something that brokers should consider. It is fairly common nowadays to have mentoring programs as a way of showing an agent the ropes of the business and the organization. But it can be more than that:

[Mentoring] should be put firmly into the service of
goodness in the business. People need good training.
But more importantly, we need good people.

If you are in an executive position, then make sure you
hire good people and do whatever you can to apprentice
them to wiser people, because by association with sages
they will catch the spirit of those values that alone can
move an organization further along the road of enduring
excellence.[49]

There is also the same advice to brokers as there is to agents. If a real
estate office becomes a place where "little acts of kindness" are practiced routinely, where friendliness and cheerfulness are the norm—and
where rudeness and mean-spiritedness are out of place—then the moral
dimension of its agents will be nurtured, and they can be expected to
do what is right in the "big" situations. Morris says: "The stories we
tell co-workers, the things we praise, the actions we reward, all contribute toward establishing the right or wrong kind of corporate spirit.
Little things make all the difference."[50]

Finally, a broker needs to have a program—a plan that is just as carefully conceived as any marketing campaign—that reinforces the values
of the company. Our priorities are revealed in our actions. Ask a
simple question: How much in the way of time and resources does the
company devote to training in the skills and methods required for
productivity? Then ask: How much in the way of time and resources
does the company devote to reinforcing its values and the importance
of ethical behavior? Generally, the answer to the latter question will be
"not much, if anything at all."

There are explanations for this. One of them is this: *Real estate firms
don't conduct their own ethics programs because they believe it is the job of the*

---

[49] Tom Morris, *If Aristotle Ran General Motors*, New York, Owl Books, Henry
Holt and Company, 1998, 163.

[50] From the same book, 165.

Realtor® organizations to teach and promote ethical conduct.

This is understandable. For years the national, state, and local Realtor® organizations have represented themselves both to their members and to the public as, so to speak, the guardians of professional morality for the real estate industry. They have, with great sincerity, taken on the tasks of defining, teaching, and enforcing rules of professional ethics for real estate practitioners.

Perhaps this worked once. But it doesn't work now. For one thing, it is a plain, albeit regrettable, fact that the activities and priorities of the Realtor® organizations are far removed from the consciousness of most agents. Second, the quadrennial mandatory ethical training required by the National Association of Realtors® is simply too infrequent an occurrence to have a real impact on most members. Finally, and of the greatest importance, questions of ethics are widely perceived to be "the Realtor® Board's issues," not those of the agent's firm. That has to change.

"But how?" a broker might reasonably ask. "I don't know how to teach about ethics; and neither does my staff." There are some encouraging signs that help is on the way:

(1) At the 2006 midyear meetings of the National Association of Realtors®, directors approved a budget augmentation for the purpose of developing twenty (later reduced to fifteen) 4- to 6-minute videostreamed training modules discussing ethical principles. These will also be available in DVD format near the end of 2007. They will be widely distributed and will enhance the ability of brokers to provide ethics training on-site. With this program, NAR will, in effect, be creating lesson plans for use by individual brokerages. It will provide real estate companies with a great opportunity to provide ongoing ethics training to their agents. It will give them the means to demonstrate their professed commitments.

(2) In 2006 the Realtor® Association of West/South Suburban Chicagoland (RWSSC, also known as MainStreet Organization of Realtors®) produced a video, *Pathways to Professionalism*, that deals with

the not-always-common courtesies and behaviors that make up so much of what is called "professionalism." This video is based on a document of the same name that was originally produced by a Professional Conduct Work Group of NAR in 1998. It was subsequently updated by the Professional Standards Committee and approved by the NAR Board of Directors in 2004.

The video focuses on what some might think are the "little things." But, as we have noted, the so-called "little things" are vitally important. There is a great deal of overlap in the areas of manners and morals (or, if you like, courtesy and right action), where both are informed by the Golden Rule. The principle behind "return your phone calls" and "let people know if you're running late" is the same as that which undergirds injunctions to tell the truth and to treat others fairly. It is the Golden Rule, the principle of treating others as we would want to be treated. *Pathways to Professionalism* is available to individual brokers, and it offers a good starting point to those who want to foster an ethical climate in their office.

(3) Recently, the Virginia Association of Realtors® (VAR) has undertaken an innovative project to provide ethics training and material that can be accessed by individual brokers and agents. VAR created a website (www.tedtruitt.com) that features an over-the-top character, Ted Truitt, who is the very embodiment of what we might call the "anti-ethical." Using this humor, they point to their real website, www.thecodeisgoodbusiness, which provides plain-language talk about the Realtor® Code of Ethics, postings of articles about ethical issues related to real estate, and a variety of resources and materials.

So, there is help for brokers who would like to see ethics training in their offices but who feel they lack the resources. But even if nothing were available, they should still not be reluctant to start. If they would just bring up situations familiar to many of us—stories like the ones throughout this text—they will find that everyone will have thoughts to contribute and there will be plenty to talk about.

Appendices

APPENDIX 1

Excerpts From HUD's Policy Statement on Sham Controlled Business Arrangements
(Federal Register: June 7,1996 [Volume 61, Number 111])
http://www.hud.gov/offices/hsg/sfh/res/res0607c.cfm

*SUMMARY: This statement sets forth the factors that the Department uses to determine whether a controlled business arrangement is a sham under the Real Estate Settlement Procedures Act (**RESPA**) or whether it constitutes a bona fide provider of settlement services. It provides an interpretation of the legislative and regulatory framework for HUD's enforcement practices involving sham arrangements that do not come within the definition of and exception for controlled business arrangements under Sections 3(7) and 8(c)(4) of the Real Estate Settlement Procedures Act (**RESPA**). It is published to give guidance and to inform interested members of the public of the Department's interpretation of this section of the law.*

***

General Background
Section 8 (a) of the Real Estate Settlement Procedures Act (**RESPA**) prohibits any person from giving or accepting any fee, kickback, or thing of value for the referral of settlement service business involving a federally related mortgage loan. 12 U.S.C. Sec. 2607(a). Congress specifically stated it intended to eliminate kickbacks and referral fees that tend to increase unnecessarily the costs of settlement services. 12 U.S.C. Sec. 2601(b)(2).

   After **RESPA**'s passage, the Department received many questions asking if referrals between affiliated settlement service providers violated **RESPA**. Congress held hearings in 1981. In 1983, Congress amended **RESPA** to permit controlled business arrangements (CBAs) under certain conditions, while retaining the general prohibitions against the giving and taking of referral fees. Congress defined the term "controlled business arrangement" to mean an arrangement:

[I]n which (A) a person who is in a position to refer business incident to or a part of a real estate settlement service involving a federally related mortgage loan, or an associate of such person, has either an affiliate relationship with or a direct or beneficial ownership interest of more than 1 percent in a provider of settlement services; and (B) either of such persons directly or indirectly refers such business to that provider or affirmatively influences the selection of that provider.

12 U.S.C. 2602(7) (emphasis added).

In November 1992, HUD issued its first regulation covering controlled business arrangements, 57 FR 49599 (Nov. 2, 1992), codified at 24 CFR 3500.15. <SUP>1 That rule provided that a controlled business arrangement was not a violation of Section 8 and allowed referrals of business to an affiliated settlement service provider so long as: (1) The consumer receives a written disclosure of the nature of the relationship and an estimate of the affiliate's charges; (2) the consumer is not required to use the controlled entity; and (3) the only thing of value received from the arrangement, other than payments for services rendered, is a return on ownership interest.

***

Congress did not intend for the controlled business arrangement ("CBA") amendment to be used to promote referral fee payments through sham arrangements or shell entities. H.R. Rep. 123, 98th Cong., 1st Sess. 76 (1983). The CBA definition addresses associations between providers of settlement services. 12 U.S.C. 2602(7). In order to come within the CBA exception, the entity receiving the referrals of settlement service business must be a "provider" of settlement service business. If the entity is not a bona fide provider of settlement services, then the arrangement does not meet the definition of a CBA. If an arrangement does not meet the definition of a CBA, it cannot qualify for the CBA exception, even if the three conditions of Section 8(c) are otherwise met. 12 U.S.C. 2607(c)(4)(A-C). Therefore, subsequent compliance with the CBA conditions concerning disclosure, non-required use and payments from the arrangement that are a return on ownership interest, will not exempt payments that flow through an entity that is not a provider of settlement services.

Thus, in **RESPA** enforcement cases involving a controlled business arrangement created by two existing settlement service providers, HUD considers whether the entity receiving referrals of business (regardless of legal structure) is a bona fide provider of settlement services. When assessing whether such an entity is a bona fide provider of settlement services or is merely a sham arrangement used as a conduit for referral fee payments, HUD balances a number of factors in determining whether a violation exists and whether an enforcement action under Section 8 is appropriate. Responses to the questions below will be considered together in determining whether the entity is a bona fide settlement service provider. A response to any one question by itself may not be determinative of a sham controlled business arrangement. The Department will consider the following factors and will weigh them in light of the specific facts in determining whether an entity is a bona fide provider:

(1) Does the new entity have sufficient initial capital and net worth, typical in the industry, to conduct the settlement service business for which it was created? Or is it undercapitalized to do the work it purports to provide?

(2) Is the new entity staffed with its own employees to perform the services it provides? Or does the new entity have "loaned" employees of one of the parent providers?

(3) Does the new entity manage its own business affairs? Or is an entity that helped create the new entity running the new entity for the parent provider making the referrals?

(4) Does the new entity have an office for business which is separate from one of the parent providers? If the new entity is located at the same business address as one of the parent providers, does the new entity pay a general market value rent for the facilities actually furnished?

(5) Is the new entity providing substantial services, i.e., the essential functions of the real estate settlement service, for which the entity receives a fee? Does it incur the risks and receive the rewards of any comparable enterprise operating in the market place?

(6) Does the new entity perform all of the substantial services itself? Or does it contract out part of the work? If so, how much of the work is contracted out?

(7) If the new entity contracts out some of its essential functions, does it contract services from an independent third party? Or are the

services contracted from a parent, affiliated provider or an entity that helped create the controlled entity? If the new entity contracts out work to a parent, affiliated provider or an entity that helped create it, does the new entity provide any functions that are of value to the settlement process?

(8) If the new entity contracts out work to another party, is the party performing any contracted services receiving a payment for services or facilities provided that bears a reasonable relationship to the value of the services or goods received? Or is the contractor providing services or goods at a charge such that the new entity is receiving a "thing of value" for referring settlement service business to the party performing the service?

(9) Is the new entity actively competing in the market place for business? Does the new entity receive or attempt to obtain business from settlement service providers other than one of the settlement service providers that created the new entity?

(10) Is the new entity sending business exclusively to one of the settlement service providers that created it (such as the title application for a title policy to a title insurance underwriter or a loan package to a lender)? Or does the new entity send business to a number of entities, which may include one of the providers that created it?

Even if an entity is a bona fide provider of settlement services, that finding does not end the inquiry. Questions may still exist as to whether the entity complies with the three conditions of the controlled business arrangement exception.

***

Some examples of how HUD will use these factors in an analysis of specific circumstances are provided below.

Examples:

1. An existing real estate broker and an existing title insurance company form a joint venture title agency. Each participant in the joint venture contributes $1000 towards the creation of the joint venture title agency, which will be an exclusive agent for the title insurance company. The title insurance company enters a service agreement with the joint venture to provide title search, examination and title commitment preparation work at a charge lower than its cost. It also provides the management for the joint venture. The joint venture is located in the title insurance company's office space. One employee of the title insurance company is "leased" to the joint

venture to handle closings and prepare policies. That employee continues to do the same work she did for the title insurance company. The real estate broker participant is the joint venture's sole source of business referrals. Profits of the joint venture are divided equally between the real estate broker and title insurance company.

HUD Analysis. After reviewing all of the factors, HUD would consider this an example of an entity which is not a bona fide provider of settlement service business. As such, the payments flowing through the arrangement are not exempt under Section 8(c)(4) and would be subject to further analysis under Section 8. In looking at the amount of capitalization used to create the settlement service business, it appears that the entity is undercapitalized to perform the work of a full service title agency. In this example, although there is an equal contribution of capital, the title insurance company is providing much of the title insurance work, office space and management oversight for the venture to operate. Although the venture has an employee, the employee is leased from and continues to be supervised by the title insurance company. This new entity receives all the referrals of business from the real estate broker participant and does not compete for business in the market place. The venture provides a few of the essential functions of a title agent, but it contracts many of the core title agent functions to the title insurance company. In addition, the title insurance company provides the search, examination and title commitment work at less than its cost, so it may be seen as providing a "thing of value" to the referring title agent, which is passed on to the real estate broker participant in a return on ownership.

2. A title insurance company solicits a real estate broker to create a company wholly owned by the broker to act as its title agent. The title insurance company sets up the new company for the real estate broker. It also manages the new company, which is staffed by its former employees that continue to do their former work. As in the previous example, the new company also contracts back certain of the core title agent services from the title insurance company that created it, including the examination and determination of insurability of title, and preparation of the title insurance commitment. The title insurance company charges the new company less that its costs for these services. The new company's employees conduct the closings and issue only policies of title insurance on behalf of the title insurance company that created it.

HUD Analysis. As was the case in the first example, HUD would not consider the new entity to be a bona fide settlement service provider. The legal structure of the new entity is irrelevant. The new company does little real work and contracts back a substantial part of the core work to the title insurance company that set it up. Further, the employees of the new company continue to do the work they previously did for the title insurance company which also continues to manage the employees. The new entity is not competing for business in the market place. All of the referrals of business to the new entity come from the real estate broker owner. The creating title insurance company provides the bulk of the title work. On balance HUD would consider these factors and find that the new entity is not a bona fide title agent, and the payments flowing through the arrangement are not exempt under Section 8(c)(4) and would be subject to further analysis under Section 8.

3. A lender and a real estate broker form a joint venture mortgage broker. The real estate broker participant in the joint venture does not require its prospective home buyers to use the new entity and it provides the required CBA disclosures at the time of the referral. The real estate broker participant is the sole source of the joint venture's business. The lender and real estate broker each contributes an equal amount of capital towards the joint venture, which represents a sufficient initial capital investment and which is typical in the industry. The new entity, using its own employees, prepares loan applications and performs all other functions of a mortgage broker. On a few occasions, to accommodate surges in business, the new entity contracts out some of the loan processing work to third party providers, including the lender participant in the joint venture. In these cases, the new entity pays all third party providers a similar fee, which is reasonably related to the processing work performed. The new entity manages its own business affairs. It rents space in the real estate participant's office at the general market rate. The new entity submits loan applications to numerous lenders and only a small percent goes to the lender participant in the joint venture.

HUD Analysis. After reviewing all of the factors, HUD would consider this an example of an entity which is a bona fide provider of settlement service business rather than a sham arrangement. The new entity would appear to have sufficient capital to perform the services of a mortgage broker. The participant's interests appear to be based on a fair value contribution and free from tie-ins to referrals of business. The new entity has its own staff and manages its own business. While it shares a business address with the real estate broker participant, it pays a fair market rent for that space. It provides substantial mortgage brokerage services. Even though the joint venture may contract out some processing overflow to its lender participant, this work does not represent a substantial portion of the mortgage brokerage services provided by the joint venture. Moreover, the joint venture pays all third party providers a similar fee for similar processing services.

While the real estate broker participant is the sole source of referrals to the venture, the venture only sends a small percent of its loan business to the lender participant. The joint venture mortgage broker is thus actively referring loan business to lenders other than its lender participant. Since the real estate broker provides the CBA disclosure and does not require the use of the mortgage broker and the only return to the participants is based on the profits of the venture and not reflective of referrals made to the venture, it meets the CBA exemption requirements. HUD would consider this a bona fide controlled business arrangement.

4. A real estate brokerage company decides that it wishes to expand its operations into the title insurance business. Based on a fair value contribution, it purchases from a title insurance company a 50 percent ownership interest in an existing full service title agency that does business in its area. The title agency is liable for the core title services it provides, which includes conducting the title searches, evaluating the title search to determine the insurability of title, clearing underwriting objections, preparing title commitments, conducting the closing, and issuing the title policy. The agent is an exclusive title agent for its title insurance company owner. Under the new ownership, the real estate brokerage company does not require its prospective home buyers to use its title agency. The brokerage has its real estate agents provide the required CBA disclosures when the home buyer is referred to the affiliated title insurance agency. The real estate brokerage company is not the sole source of the title agency's business. The real estate brokerage company receives a return on ownership in proportion to its 50% ownership interest and unrelated to referrals of business.

HUD Analysis. A review of the factors reflects an arrangement involving a bona fide provider of settlement services. In this example, the real estate brokerage company is not the sole source of referrals to the title agency. However, the title agency continues its exclusive agency arrangement with the title insurance company owner. While this last factor initially may raise a question as to why other title insurance companies are not used for title insurance policies, upon review there appears to be nothing impermissible about these referrals of title business from the title agency to the title insurance company.

This example involves the purchase of stock in an existing full service provider. In such a situation, HUD would carefully examine the investment made by the real estate brokerage company. In this example, the real estate brokerage company pays a fair value contribution for its ownership share and receives a return on its investment that is not based on referrals of business. Since the real estate brokerage provides the CBA disclosure, does not require the use of the title agency and the only return to the brokerage is based on the profits of the agency and not reflective of referrals made, the arrangement meets the CBA exemption requirements. HUD would consider this a bona fide controlled business arrangement.

5. A mortgage banker sets up a limited liability mortgage brokerage company. The mortgage banker sells shares in divisions of the limited liability company to real estate brokers and real estate agents. For $500 each, the real estate brokers and agents may purchase separate "divisions" within the limited liability mortgage brokerage company to which they refer customers for loans. In later years ownership may vary by the amount of referrals made by a real estate broker or agent in the previous year. Under this structure, the ownership distributions are based on the business each real estate broker or real estate agent refers to his/her division and not on the basis of their capital contribution to the entity as a whole. The limited liability mortgage brokerage company provides all the substantial services of a mortgage broker. It does not contract out any processing to its mortgage banker owner. It sends loan packages to its mortgage banker owner as well as other lenders.

HUD analysis. Although HUD would consider the mortgage brokerage company to be a bona fide provider of mortgage brokerage services, this example illustrates an arrangement that fails to meet the third condition of the CBA exception. 12 U.S.C. 2607(c)(4)(C). Here, the capitalization, ownership and payment structure with ownership in separate "divisions" is a method in which ownership returns or ownership shares vary based on referrals made and not on the amount contributed to the capitalization of the company. In cases where the percent of ownership interest or the amount of payment varies by the amount of business the real estate agent or broker refers, such payments are not bona fide returns on ownership interest, but instead, are an indirect method of paying a kickback based on the amount of business referred. 24 CFR 3500.15(b)(3).

Authority: 12 U.S.C. 2617; 42 U.S.C. 3535(d).

Dated: May 31, 1996.

Nicolas P. Retsinas,

Assistant Secretary for Housing-Federal Housing Commissioner.

APPENDIX 2
12 USC Section 2607
Prohibition against Kickbacks and Unearned Fees

From the U.S. Code Online via GPO Access [wais.access.gpo.gov]
[Laws in effect as of January 27, 1998] [Document not affected by Public Laws
enacted between January 27, 1998 and November 30, 1998]
[CITE: 12USC2607]

TITLE 12–BANKS AND BANKING
CHAPTER 27–REAL ESTATE SETTLEMENT PROCEDURES

Sec. 2607. Prohibition against kickbacks and unearned fees

(a) Business referrals

No person shall give and no person shall accept any fee, kickback, or thing of value pursuant to any agreement or understanding,
oral or otherwise, that business incident to or a part of a real estate
settlement service involving a federally related mortgage loan shall be
referred to any person.

(b) Splitting charges

No person shall give and no person shall accept any portion,
split, or percentage of any charge made or received for the rendering of
a real estate settlement service in connection with a transaction
involving a federally related mortgage loan other than for services
actually performed.

(c) Fees, salaries, compensation, or other payments

Nothing in this section shall be construed as prohibiting (1) the
payment of a fee (A) to attorneys at law for services actually rendered
or (B) by a title company to its duly appointed agent for services
actually performed in the issuance of a policy of title insurance or (C)
by a lender to its duly appointed agent for services actually performed
in the making of a loan, (2) the payment to any person of a bona fide
salary or compensation or other payment for goods or facilities actually
furnished or for services actually performed, (3) payments pursuant to
cooperative brokerage and referral arrangements or agreements
between real estate agents and brokers, (4) affiliated business arrangements so long as (A) a disclosure is made of the existence of such an
arrangement to the person being referred and, in connection with
such referral, such person is provided a written estimate of the charge
or range of charges generally made by the provider to which the person

is referred (i) in the case of a face-to-face referral or a referral made in writing or by electronic media, at or before the time of the referral (and compliance with this requirement in such case may be evidenced by a notation in a written, electronic, or similar system of records maintained in the regular course of business); (ii) in the case of a referral made by telephone, within 3 business days after the referral by telephone,\1\ (and in such case an abbreviated verbal disclosure of the existence of the arrangement and the fact that a written disclosure will be provided within 3 business days shall be made to the person being referred during the telephone referral); or (iii) in the case of a referral by a lender (including a referral by a lender to an affiliated lender), at the time the estimates required under section 2604(c) of this title are provided (notwithstanding clause (i) or (ii)); and any required written receipt of such disclosure (without regard to the manner of the disclosure under clause (i), (ii), or (iii)) may be obtained at the closing or settlement (except that a person making a face-to-face referral who provides the written disclosure at or before the time of the referral shall attempt to obtain any required written receipt of such disclosure at such time and if the person being referred chooses not to acknowl-edge the receipt of the disclosure at that time, that fact shall be noted in the written, electronic, or similar system of records maintained in the regular course of business by the person making the referral), (B) such person is not required to use any particular provider of settlement services, and (C) the only thing of value that is received from the arrangement, other than the payments permitted under this subsec-tion, is a return on the ownership interest or franchise relationship, or (5) such other payments or classes of payments or other transfers as are specified in regulations prescribed by the Secretary, after consultation with the Attorney General, the Secretary of Veterans Affairs, the Federal Home Loan Bank Board, the Federal Deposit Insurance Corporation, the Board of Governors of the Federal Reserve System, and the Secretary of Agriculture. For purposes of the preceding sentence, the following shall not be considered a violation of clause (4)(B): (i) any arrangement that requires a buyer, borrower, or seller to pay for the services of an attorney, credit reporting agency, or real estate appraiser chosen by the lender to represent the lender's interest in a real estate transaction, or (ii) any arrangement where an attorney or law firm represents a client in a real estate transaction and issues or arranges for the issuance of a policy of title insurance in the transac-tion directly as agent or through a separate corporate title insurance agency that may be established by that attorney or law firm and operated as an adjunct to his or its law practice.

\1\ So in original.

(d) Penalties for violations; joint and several liability; treble damages; actions for injunction by Secretary and by State officials; costs and attorney fees; construction of State laws
(1) Any person or persons who violate the provisions of this section shall be fined not more than $10,000 or imprisoned for not more than one year, or both.
(2) Any person or persons who violate the prohibitions or limitations of this section shall be jointly and severally liable to the person or persons charged for the settlement service involved in the violation in an amount equal to three times the amount of any charge paid for such settlement service.
(3) No person or persons shall be liable for a violation of the provisions of subsection (c)(4)(A) of this section if such person or persons proves by a preponderance of the evidence that such violation was not intentional and resulted from a bona fide error notwithstanding maintenance of procedures that are reasonably adapted to avoid such error.
(4) The Secretary, the Attorney General of any State, or the insurance commissioner of any State may bring an action to enjoin violations of this section.
(5) In any private action brought pursuant to this subsection, the court may award to the prevailing party the court costs of the action together with reasonable attorneys fees.
(6) No provision of State law or regulation that imposes more stringent limitations on affiliated business arrangements shall be construed as being inconsistent with this section.
(Pub. L. 93-533, Sec. 8, Dec. 22, 1974, 88 Stat. 1727; Pub. L. 94-205, Sec. 7, Jan. 2, 1976, 89 Stat. 1158; Pub. L. 98-181, title IV, Sec. 461(b), (c), Nov. 30, 1983, 97 Stat. 1231; Pub. L. 100-242, title V, Sec. 570(g), Feb. 5, 1988, 101 Stat. 1950; Pub. L. 102-54, Sec. 13(d)(4), June 13, 1991, 105 Stat. 275; Pub. L. 104-208, div. A, title II, Sec. 2103(c)(2), (d), Sept. 30, 1996, 110 Stat. 3009-400.)
Amendments
1996—Subsec. (c)(4). Pub. L. 104-208, Sec. 2103(c)(2), substituted "affiliated business arrangements" for "controlled business arrangements".
Subsec. (c)(4)(A). Pub. L. 104-208, Sec. 2103(d), amended subcl. (A) generally. Prior to amendment, subcl. (A) read as follows: "at or prior

to the time of the referral a disclosure is made of the existence of such an arrangement to the person being referred and, in connection with the referral, such person is provided a written estimate of the charge or range of charges generally made by the provider to which the person is referred, except that where a lender makes the referral, this requirement may be satisfied as part of and at the time that the estimates of settlement charges required under section 2604(c) of this title are provided,".

Subsec. (d)(6). Pub. L. 104-208, Sec. 2103(c)(2), substituted "affiliated business arrangements" for "controlled business arrangements".

1991—Subsec. (c)(5). Pub. L. 102-54 substituted "Secretary of Veterans Affairs" for "Administrator of Veterans' Affairs".

1988—Subsec. (c)(5). Pub. L. 100-242 substituted "clause (4)(B)" for "clause 4(B)".

1983—Subsec. (c). Pub. L. 98-181, Sec. 461(b), redesignated cl. (4) as (5), added cl. (4) and provisions following cl. (5), as so redesignated, relating to arrangements which shall not be considered a violation of cl. (4)(B).

Subsec. (d)(2). Pub. L. 98-181, Sec. 461(c), substituted provisions setting forth the liability of persons violating the prohibitions or limitations of this section for provisions setting forth liability, in addition to penalties provided in par. (1), of persons violating subsecs. (a) and (b) of this section, plus costs and attorney's fees.

Subsec. (d)(3) to (6). Pub. L. 98-181, Sec. 461(c), added pars. (3) to (6).

1976—Subsec. (c). Pub. L. 94-205 added cls. (3) and (4).

Effective Date of 1983 Amendment

Amendment by Pub. L. 98-181 effective Jan. 1, 1984, see section 461(f) of Pub. L. 98-181, set out as a note under section 2602 of this title.

Effective Date of 1976 Amendment

Amendment by Pub. L. 94-205 effective Jan. 2, 1976, see section 12 of Pub. L. 94-205, set out as a note under section 2602 of this title.

Transfer of Functions

Federal Home Loan Bank Board abolished and functions transferred, see sections 401 to 406 of Pub. L. 101-73, set out as a note under section 1437 of this title.

Section Referred to in Other Sections

This section is referred to in section 2614 of this title.

U.S. Department of Housing and Urban Development

451 7th Street, S.W., Washington, DC 20410

Telephone: (202) 708-1112.

APPENDIX 3
FAIR HOUSING ADVERTISING WORD AND PHRASE LIST
Revised 05/15/06

This word and phrase list is intended as a guideline to assist in complying with state and federal fair housing laws. It is not intended as a complete list of every word or phrase that could violate any local, state, or federal statutes.

This list is intended to educate and provide general guidance to the many businesses in the Miami Valley that create and publish real estate advertising. This list is not intended to provide legal advice. By its nature, a general list cannot cover particular persons' situations or questions. The list is intended to make you aware of and sensitive to the important legal obligations concerning discriminatory real estate advertising.

For additional information, contact the Miami Valley Fair Housing Center at (937) 223-6035.

BOLD — not acceptable
ITALIC — caution
STANDARD — acceptable

able-bodied
Active
adult community
adult living
adult park
adults only
African, no
Agile
AIDS, no
Alcoholics, no
Appalachian, no
American Indians, no
Asian
Assistance animal(s)
Assistance animal(s) only
Bachelor
Bachelor pad
Blacks, no
blind, no
board approval required
Catholic
Caucasian
Chicano, no
children, no
Chinese

Christian
Churches, near
college students, no
Colored Congregation
Convalescent home Convenient to
Couple
couples only
Credit check required
crippled, no
Curfew
Deaf, no
Den
disabled, no
domestics, quarters
Drug users, no
Drugs, no
employed, must be
empty nesters
English only
Equal Housing Opportunity
ethnic references
Exclusive
Executive

BOLD — not acceptable ITALIC — caution <u>STANDARD — acceptable</u>

families, no
<u>families welcome</u>
<u>family room</u>
<u>family, great for</u>
female roommate**
female(s) only**
55 and older community*
<u>fixer-upper</u>
<u>gated community</u>
Gays, no
Gender
golden-agers only
<u>golf course, near</u>
group home(s) no
<u>guest house</u>
<u>handicap accessible</u>
handicap parking, no
Handicapped, not for
healthy only
Hindu
Hispanic, no
HIV, no
housing for older persons/seniors*
Hungarian, no
Ideal for ... (should not describe people)
impaired, no
Indian, no
Integrated
Irish, no
Italian, no
Jewish
<u>kids welcome</u>
Landmark reference
Latino, no
Lesbians, no
male roommate**
males(s) only**
man (men) only**
Mature
mature complex
mature couple
mature individuals
mature person(s)
<u>membership available</u>
Membership approval required
Mentally handicapped, no
Mentally ill, no
Mexican, no

Mexican-American, no
Migrant workers, no
Mormon Temple
Mosque
<u>Mother-in-law apartment</u>
Muslim
Nanny's room
Nationality
Near
Negro, no
<u>Neighborhood name</u>
Newlyweds
<u>Nice</u>
non- smokers
<u># of bedrooms</u>
# of children
# of persons
<u># of sleeping areas</u>
<u>Nursery</u>
<u>nursing home</u>
Older person(s)
one child
one person
Oriental, no
Parish
perfect for ...(should not describe people)
<u>pets limited to assistance animals</u>
pets, no
Philippine or Philippinos, no
physically fit
play area, no
preferred community
Prestigious
<u>Privacy</u>
Private
<u>Private driveway</u>
<u>Private entrance</u>
<u>Private property</u>
<u>Private setting</u>
<u>Public transportation(near)</u>
Puerto Rican, no
<u>Quality construction</u>
quality neighborhood
<u>Quiet</u>
<u>Quiet neighborhood</u>
<u>references required</u>
religious references
<u>Responsible</u>

BOLD — not acceptable   ITALIC — caution   <u>STANDARD — acceptable</u>

Restricted
retarded, no
Retirees
Retirement home
safe neighborhood
school name or school district
<u>se habla espanol</u>
<u>seasonal rates</u>
<u>seasonal worker(s), no</u>
Secluded
<u>section 8 accepted/ welcome</u>
section 8, no
Secure
<u>security provided</u>
*senior adult community**
*senior citizen(s)**
senior discount
*senior housing**
*senior(s)**
*sex or gender***
Shrine
<u>single family home</u>
single person
*single woman, man***
singles only
*sixty-two and older community**
<u>Smoker(s), no</u>
<u>Smoking, no</u>

*Snowbirds**
<u>sober</u>
Sophisticated
<u>Spanish speaking</u>
Spanish speaking, no
<u>Square feet</u>
Straight only
<u>student(s)</u>
Students, no
Supplemental Security Income (SSI), no
Synagogue, near
temple, near
tenant (description of)
<u>Townhouse</u>
traditional neighborhood
<u>traditional style</u>
tranquil setting
two people
Unemployed, no
<u>Verifiable Income</u>
walking distance of, within
Wheelchairs, no
White
White(s) only
<u>winter rental rates</u>
*winter/summer visitors**
*woman (women) only***

* Permitted to be used only when complex or development qualifies as housing for older persons

** Permitted to be used only when describing shared living areas or dwelling units used exclusively as dormitory facilities by educational institutions.

All cautionary words are unacceptable if utilized in a context that states an unlawful preference or limitation. <u>Furthermore, all cautionary words are "red flags" to fair housing enforcement agencies. Use of these words will only serve to invite further investigation and/or testing.</u>

This word and phrase list is intended as a guideline to assist in complying with state and federal fair housing laws. <u>It is not intended as a complete list of every word or phrase that could violate any local, state, or federal statutes.</u>

This list is intended to educate and provide general guidance to the many businesses in the Miami Valley that create and publish real estate advertising. <u>This list is not intended to provide legal advice. If you are in need of legal advice, please see an attorney.</u> By its nature, a general list cannot cover particular persons' situations or questions. The list is intended to make you aware of and sensitive to the important legal obligations concerning discriminatory real estate advertising.

Index of Topics